Benefiting the Child Abuse Prevention Councils of Sacramento, Placer and San Joaquin Counties.

Credits

This book was made possible by the special efforts of the following individuals:

John-Ann Carlile and Bill Donaldson of the Child Abuse Prevention Council of Sacramento, Inc., Lisa Lundquist and Cynder Sinclair of the Child Abuse Prevention Council of San Joaquin County, Brooke Allison and Pam Nelson of the Child Abuse Prevention Council of Placer County.

Special thanks to Gary Calistro at IGA and Jan Outlar Edwards from Gottschalks.

Madelynn Bruegger's ongoing persistence in organizing this project was the difference in making our work successful. Additionally, the commitment and expertise of graphic designer Mike Alie delivered the high quality represented in our publication.

Special thanks to Ron Longinotti, Claudia Johnson, Arne Jensen, Ernest Gordon, Traci Rockefeller, Kathleen Baylies, Jim Giffen, Jason Metzger, Carol Rushton, Caryn Lilley, John Koerperich, Kim Richardson, Dave and Tori Bender, Amy Lewis, Guy Farris, Maureen Reagan, Nixa Schell, The Plumbery, Andiamo, Il Fornio Panificio, Ricci's, Chuck Bolkcom, and Barclay Curtis and George Southern from Multi-Media Marketing.

Chuck Miller and Michael Himovitz of the Michael Himovitz Gallery in Sacramento provided invaluable guidance in selecting the works of several local artists, including:

Front Cover:
Roy Tellefson, Butte Summer, 1992, oil on canvas, 42" x 60"

Back Cover:
Robert Else, Spring In Winter, 1990, acrylic on canvas, 12" x 16" (courtesy D.R. Wagner collection)

The other local artists include Ron Paulat, Robin Giustina, and Joseph Bellacera.
The black and white food illustrations are by Kristine Mays.

Published in 1994 by KXTV-10, Sacramento, California.

ISBN 0-9643181-0-5

Recipe Disclaimer: The recipes included in our book were contributed by participating cooks, therefore KXTV-10 and the Child Abuse Prevention Councils do not guarantee the quality of any of the recipes. The use of brand names in recipes does not constitute an endorsement of those products by the contributing cook.

Background

California Heartland Recipes is a special project developed by KXTV-10, the CBS affiliate in Sacramento-Stockton-Modesto. The purpose of this book is two-fold: first, we wanted it to reflect the flavor and diversity of the Central Valley. Within these pages you'll discover delectable recipes from more than 250 local celebrities, chefs, and people from throughout the region. You'll also enjoy beautiful full-color reproductions of artwork depicting many of the wonderful scenic vistas of the California heartland. All of the featured artwork was created by local artists from the Michael Himovitz Gallery in Sacramento.

Second, KXTV-10 has a long-standing commitment to addressing children's issues through our "For Kids' Sake" program. We saw *California Heartland Recipes* as an opportunity to assist with those efforts. Proceeds from the sale of this book will benefit the Child Abuse Prevention Councils of Sacramento, Placer, and San Joaquin Counties. These councils work to improve the lives of children through a variety of efforts including educational and community programs, and one-on-one interaction with abused children. An overview of each council's history and mission can be found on pages viii through xiii.

We hope you enjoy the hundreds of recipes in *California Heartland Recipes* for years to come.

Robert Else
"Nature and Farming", 1990
acrylic on canvas, 24" x 36"

Table of Contents

Appetizers

Soups & Salads

Breads

Ron Paulat
"Seven Mile", 1993
oil pastel on paper, 30" x 40"

Dear Friend:

After many months of partnering with the Child Abuse Prevention Councils of Sacramento, Placer and San Joaquin Counties, dozens of local celebrities and chefs and many, many cooks from throughout our area, KXTV-10 is pleased to present *California Heartland Recipes.*

KXTV 10
400 Broadway
Sacramento CA
95818

916 441-2345

Proceeds from this effort will enable the Child Abuse Prevention Councils to expand their vital efforts in making life better for our children. Each of these councils is involved in many different levels of communinity involvement including intervention, education, grass-roots organizing, education and legislation.

We'd like to thank the two main sponsors Gottschalks and the IGA Grocers of our area for their special effort. Their support has enabled KXTV-10 to distribute *California Heartland Recipes* throughout the region.

California Heartland Recipes is just one of many projects that KXTV-10 organizes to help foster the growth of children and families. Your interest in these efforts makes the difference.

Enjoy!

Dick Cable

Dick Cable
Spokesperson - KXTV's "For Kids' Sake"
Board Member - Child Abuse Council of Sacramento, Inc.

A CBS Affiliate A Subsidiary of A.H. Belo Corporation Represented Nationally by Telerep   Printed on recycled paper

**CHILD ABUSE
PREVENTION
COUNCIL**
OF SACRAMENTO, INC.

Protecting and Promoting the
Well Being of all Children

The Child Abuse Prevention Council is Sacramento's focal point for combating child abuse and neglect.

For over 15 years, the Child Abuse Prevention Council of Sacramento has provided the leadership necessary to bring service providers, civic and religious groups, concerned citizens and policy makers together to create cost effective services for Sacramento's most damaged children and families.

The Child Abuse Prevention Council is the organization that law enforcement, family service providers, schools and local citizens have turned to for leadership to develop effective solutions and model programs for abused and neglected children:

When the Family Court was overwhelmed by increasing cases of abuse, they turned to the Child Abuse Prevention Council to help develop the Court Appointed Special Advocate program (CASA) which uses volunteers as constant friends and advocates to a child who has been removed from home because of abuse or neglect.

When the District Attorneys Office and UCD Medical Center wanted to reduce the trauma of a child going through the complex legal proceedings in child sexual abuse cases they asked the Council to help develop the Multi-Disciplinary Interview Center. The program has become a model for the state.

When the Sheriff and Coroner wanted to identify health and safety issues that could prevent future child deaths or the death of a child's sibling when a death resulted from child abuse, they asked the Council to establish and staff the Child Death Review Team.

In 1988, the Board of Supervisors asked the Child Abuse Council to convene and develop The Children's Agenda, a coalition of providers and local citizens, to plan and advocate for services to meet all our children's needs. The group created the first "Report Card" on the status of Sacramento's children, and has developed policies promoting prevention and early intervention that have been adopted by the Board of Supervisors.

In 1991, the Child Abuse Prevention Council began developing Children's Councils, self-help action teams comprised of parents and family service organizations dedicated to improving the lives of children in their neighborhoods. These groups have obtained medical services for local children and their families, created drug free zones, and organized local tenants in some of the highest crime areas in the county to improve the health and safety of their children.

The Child Abuse Prevention Council also brings families together and promotes the well-being of children through community awareness campaigns.

The Care for Our Children Holiday Campaign provides gifts to Sacramento's most vulnerable children during the holiday season and raises money for organizations working with child abuse victims. Kid's Day, one of Northern California's largest free events, provides children a chance to play and parents an opportunity to learn new ways to cope with the stress of parenting. Summer Hunger Challenge mobilizes selected neighborhoods to provide feeding, recreation and child abuse prevention education programs for children during the summer months.

"A child is a person who is going to carry on what you have started. He is going to sit where you are sitting, and when you are gone, attend to those things which you think are important. You may adopt all the policies you please, but how they are carried out depends on him. He is going to move in and take over your churches, schools, universities, and corporations...The fate of humanity is in his hands."
-Abraham Lincoln

"If we expect the children to be OUR future, and the future to be a time and place FOR our children...we must open our eyes and get to work. There is no future if we pass a damaged world to injured children. We have to rescue and love children who have become victims of abuse."
-Dick Cable
KXTV "For Kids' Sake" Spokesperson

Child Abuse Prevention Council of Sacramento, Inc.
(916) 920-1765

Robin Giustina
"Highland Lake Campsite", 1993
watercolor, 30" x 22"

San Joaquin County
Child Abuse Prevention Council

The young mother of three stood on the porch of the First Step Crisis Nursery, trying to explain her dilemma and keep from crying in front of her children. This distraught mom explained that she had just left her husband after he admitted molesting their four-year-old daughter. Could we take care of the children for a couple of days until she found a place to live? Did we know who she could call to report what happened? The crisis nursery worker invited the family inside as she struggled with a dilemma of her own: the nursery was already full for the day, with a limit of 12 children. Where would they go if the nursery turned them away for lack of space?

When families are in crisis, they are not concerned with time limits, licensing standards, boundaries and guidelines; they need help and they need it now. The nursery worker had the mother fill out the necessary paperwork and sat the children down at the table for a snack. "You go do what you need to do for your family," said the worker. "We'll take good care of them."

Adults who abuse their children are often reacting to their own past childhood experiences of abuse. Overwhelming problems and stress can trigger these abusive responses learned from their own parents. Child abuse transcends all cultural, racial, sexual and economic barriers. Sadly, child abuse plagues children from every socio-economic group.

Since 1978, the Child Abuse Prevention Council (CAPC) has provided programs and services to prevent and intervene in cases of child abuse in San Joaquin County. Striving to break the cycle of abuse, the Council intervenes in the early stages of family crisis and provides community education and awareness of child abuse prevention. A 21-member Board of Directors oversees the planning and development of this private, non-profit agency, while over 100 Auxiliary members conduct fundraising activities to support the Council.

Our highly-qualified, compassionate child care staff provides a welcome oasis for at-risk children whose parents just need a break from the often stressful job of raising kids. Focusing on prevention, we also provide respite care for children whose parents are working to put their lives back together by attending counseling, substance abuse sessions, or parenting classes. Many parents consider our child care services a key element in their recovery process. Our 24-hour facility, located on the Stockton Development Center grounds, provides free child care for children, ages birth to twelve years, for up to 10 days. We also operate a satellite nursery in Lodi.

Our Parent Education classes teach positive discipline techniques. Parents learn how to work with their children to set appropriate limits and how to enforce family rules in a positive manner. Weekly, two-hour classes comprise each 13-week session, serving both court-referred and voluntary parents. Instructors address such topics as praise and self-esteem, communication, choices and consequences, and the ages and stages of child development.

Our professional In-Home Family Service staff conducts weekly visits with families in crisis, helping them with specific concerns such as home management, budgeting, goal setting, alternative discipline techniques, and stress management. In order to learn how to provide a safer, more nurturing environment for their children, families usually need our services for six to nine months. In-Home clients include court-referred as well as self-referred families. This program owes its success to the individualized approach and tailored presentations. While we offer similar information to all clients, staff always presents it differently to each family, depending on their specific needs.

The Council also offers Prevention Services to increase community awareness through education. Our Speaker's Bureau educates the community concerning child abuse issues by addressing service clubs, churches, and businesses. In addition, Council representatives conduct signs and symptoms training sessions for local professionals, mandated by the courts to report suspected child abuse. Prevention Services also conducts video, filmstrip and puppet presentations to school-aged children to empower them to recognize and prevent child abuse, especially molest.

Each year millions of American children suffer from child abuse. Thousands die as a result. In 1993 alone, San Joaquin County received nearly 13,000 reported cases of child abuse. The situation is critical. You can become a "partner in prevention" by supporting your local Child Abuse Prevention Council. It shouldn't hurt to be a child.

San Joaquin County Child Abuse Prevention Council
(209) 464-4524

Robin Giustina
"Badminton at the Beach", 1993
acrylic on illustration board, 9" x 12"

xi

**Child Abuse
Prevention
Council**
of Placer County

The Child Abuse Prevention Council of Placer County is a not-for-profit agency formed in 1988. It is governed by community leaders and children's agency professionals devoted to preventing and healing child abuse in all its forms.

Council Goals:

• To advocate for the needs of Placer County's abused and neglected children.

• To educate professionals and the community-at-large to recognize and do something about child abuse.

• To create new programs to prevent abuse and to help abused and neglected children.

• To plan and coordinate existing children's services to make them more responsive and more cost-effective.

Council Programs and Accomplishments:

• Child Abuse and Abduction Protection Education (C.A.P.E.) program teaches Placer County's elementary school children, their parents and teachers, to recognize and defend against child abuse.

• Multi-Disciplinary Interview Center (M.D.I.C.) where child victims of sexual abuse in Placer County are interviewed by trained specialists in a child-friendly setting. Children's trauma is reduced, the truth-finding process enhanced, and successful prosecution increased to remove molesters from our streets.

• Family Cooperative Project (F.C.P.) is a community-based day care co-op, positive parenting center, and ancillary service network for low-income families at risk of child abuse.

• Court Appointed Special Advocate (C.A.S.A.) program under development to assist the juvenile court with decisions regarding the permanent removal of children from abusive homes and to provide support to children as they proceed through the dependency process.

• The Council also provides the general public and specific organizations with ongoing education, information, and referral on issues related to child abuse through our resource library, annual conferences and workshops, quarterly newsletter and Speakers' Bureau.

How Can You Make a Difference?

• Join the Council as a member to support our County's children's programs.

• Become a community volunteer for the Family Cooperative Project, CAPE or CASA.

• Become a trained member of the Council's Speakers' Bureau.

• Attend the Council's Community Education Forums to learn more about what you can do to identify and stop child abuse.

Child Abuse Prevention Council of Placer County
(916) 823-0253

Robin Giustina
"Blue Cooler", 1993
watercolor, 30" x 22"

The following IGA Grocers are proud to support the Child Abuse Prevention Councils of Sacramento, San Joaquin, and Placer Counties efforts:

Big Al's IGA
422 Main Street
Wheatland

Chung Sun IGA
110 Sixth Street
Colusa

Food Town IGA
2224 El Camino Avenue
Sacramento

Food King IGA
8626 Lower Sacramento
Stockton

Galt Super IGA
814 A Street
Galt

Food City IGA
4604 Franklin Blvd
Sacramento

SPD IGA Markets
735 Zion Street
Nevada City

SPD IGA Markets
129 McKnight Way
Grass Valley

Jumbo IGA
2355 Florin Rd
Sacramento

Lira's Supermarket IGA
609 Highway 12
Rio Vista

Jumbo IGA
5820 South Land Park Dr
Sacramento

State IGA
655 Russell Blvd
Davis

Arden Plaza IGA
4315 Arden Way
Sacramento

Town & Country IGA
121 E. Grant Ave
Winters

Village Center IGA
16985 Placer Hills Rd
Meadow Vista

Vic's IGA
1340 Fulton Avenue
Sacramento

Wells Ave. Market
1500 S Wells Ave
Reno, Nevada

Worton's IGA
23410 Forest Hill Rd
Forest Hills

Robert Else
"End", 1985
acrylic on canvas, 28" x 36"

GOTTSCHALKS
90
Years of Customer Service

Serving Our Community, Serving Our Future

Our unique and enviable California lifestyle is no accident. It is the product of a long tradition of Californians serving Californians to create a higher standard of living for all. In the same tradition, Gottschalks is constantly seeking new ways in which to contribute to an enhanced California lifestyle. Therefore, we are particularly proud to be a partner with the Child Abuse Prevention Councils of Sacramento, Placer and San Joaquin Counties in presenting *California Heartland Recipes*. This collection of favorite recipes from the kitchens of many of our better known community members will add diversity to your table and, in supporting this worthwhile cause, warmth to your soul. It is the aim of Gottschalks to provide continuing support through worthwhile community programs such as this to ensure that the lifestyle we all enjoy is preserved and enriched for ourselves and our children.

Gottschalks is pleased to serve the Sacramento area in the following locations:

Sacramento:	Country Club Plaza	**Stockton:**	Sherwood Mall
Woodland:	County Fair Mall	**Yuba City:**	Yuba City Mall
Modesto:	Century Center & Vintage Faire Mall	**Antioch:**	County East Mall

Joseph Bellacera
"Wetlands", 1991
monotype, 16" x 20"

Appetizers

Broccoli Dip

20 ounces frozen broccoli
1 large onion
4 stalks celery
2 sticks Kraft margarine or Crystal butter
2 cans cream of mushroom soup
1 pound Kraft Velveeta or American cheese

Cook frozen broccoli according to package. Drain. Place broccoli in blender along with chopped onion and celery. Mix until pasty. Saute mixture in two sticks of butter or margarine. Add cream of mushroom soup and one pound of cheese. Serve warm with tortilla chips.

Jaime Garza

Jaime Garza is an anchor/reporter at KXTV and hosts the show "Basic Colors". He got his start in television news at the University of Texas at Austin. He says his Mom deserves an award for her tasty broccoli dip!

Hot Artichoke Dip

2 cans water packed artichoke hearts
2 small cans diced green chiles
1 cup Kraft mayonnaise
1 cup Crystal sour cream
3/4 cup grated Kraft Monterey Jack cheese
1/2 cup Kraft Parmesan cheese

Drain and shred artichoke hearts. Mix all ingredients together and place in shallow baking dish. Bake 350° about 15 minutes or until golden brown. Serve hot with tortilla chips. Serves: 15-20

Deborah Pacyna

Deborah Pacyna has been a news reporter for KXTV since 1984. She is married, has 2 small children and obtained this quick and popular recipe during a neighborhood get-together. She says, "It's such a hit, I usually have copies of the recipe available when I serve it."

Fruit Dip

1 16-ounce jar marshmallow topping
1 16-ounce container sour creme
1 tablespoon orange extract

Judy Mitchell
Roseville, CA

Mix all ingredients together until smooth. Cut up bananas, pineapple, grapes, melons, apples, etc... and "dip away"!

Easy and unusual treat that always brings compliments.

19

Proscuitto Basil Wrapped Prawns

Ward Feest - Jakes On The Lake

We created this recipe in Southern California in one of our many established restaurants, it became one of our most popular appetizers. When moving to Lake Tahoe, I brought this one with me. I found it to be very successful here also.

40 black tiger prawns (5 each to order)
1/4 pound proscuitto ham sliced thin
40 basil leaves
8 skewers

Dijon Mustard Dipping Sauce:
1 ounce dijon mustard
4 ounces olive oil
3 ounces red wine vinegar
1 1/2 ounces garlic, chopped garlic
pinch salt
pinch pepper

Peel and devein prawns. Slice proscuitto ham very thin, approximately 1 inch strips. Lay basil leaf on top of proscuitto. Lay prawn on top of basil. Roll together and skewer. Charbroil. Remove skewer and set on plate with side of Dijon mustard dipping sauce.

Sauce: add mustard, garlic, red wine vinegar in blender on medium speed. Slowly add oil and salt and pepper to taste. Blend for 3 minutes. When complete, chop a little fresh spinach for garnish. Serves: 8

Spicy Pickled Asparagus

approximately 10 pounds fresh
    asparagus
10 garlic cloves
Schilling cayenne pepper
black peppercorns
10 dried, red chili peppers
fresh dill or dill seed
2 quarts cider vinegar
2 quarts water
1/2 cup pickling salt
10 wide mouth canning jars with
    rings and lids

Donna Riley Ohm
Stockton, CA

Wash and cut asparagus to 1/2 inch shorter than jar.

Add the following to each sterilized jar: 1 clove peeled garlic, 6 peppercorns, 1 dried red pepper, 1 head fresh dill or 1 teaspoon dill seed and 1/8 teaspoon cayenne pepper.

Pack asparagus tightly in jar, stem down.

Bring to boil: 2 quarts vinegar, 2 quarts water and 1/2 cup salt.

Pour hot liquid over asparagus in jars, leaving 1/4 inch head space.

Wipe rims clean and put on canning lids and rings.

Process in boiling water bath for 5 minutes. Cool.

Store jars upside down in a cool dark location. Let season 4 to 6 weeks before tasting.

Cheese Delight

Nikke Van Derheydt-Sosnick Asid

Born in Sacramento, Pursued her education in New York and Paris at the Parson School of Design. Great Knowledge and expertise in areas of design and interior design. Established her interior design firm in 1968 working in both the commercial and residential arenas and has received much recognition.

1 loaf sweet French bread
1 egg
sharp cheddar cheese
fresh bay shrimp

Cut crust off bread, cube bread - 1 1/2" squares.

Beat 1 egg, add enough grated cheese until mixture is dry or not runny, fold in shrimp.

Dip squares in mixture, coat all sides, place 1 shrimp on top of cube. Place on a non stick or greased cookie sheet.

Bake at 350° until cheese is bubbly. Serves: 12+

Chili Cheese Squares

3/4 pound grated Kraft sharp cheddar cheese
3/4 pound grated Kraft Monterey Jack cheese
1 small can green chilies, chopped
6-7 IGA California eggs, lightly beaten

Joan Mason
Stockton, CA

Lightly grease an 8" or 9" square pan. Spread all the grated cheddar over the bottom. Cover with all the green chilies, spreading them evenly. Cover with the grated jack cheese. Pour the eggs over the cheese and bake at 325° for about 1 hour. Cut into cubes and serve warm or at room temperature.

Dos Amigos Salsa (mild version for rookies)

Ron Camacho

1 cup chopped red onion
1 bunch of green onions
2 cloves of garlic
2 jalapenos (if you want it hotter, just add more)
1 cup chopped celery (try not to pulverize)
1/4 cup of white vinegar
1 tablespoon of Schilling oregano
2 #2 cans of stewed tomatoes

Blend onions, garlic and jalapenos. Add celery, vinegar and oregano, mix. Then mix in tomatoes. Makes about 3 quarts of muy bueno salsa. Mix well and refrigerate. Salsa tastes better with age and it gets hotter!

Spinach Rails

1 cup Kraft mayonnaise
1 cup Crystal sour cream
1 small package ranch dressing mix
  (powder)
1 can (6-ounce) water chestnuts,
  chopped fine
2 package frozen chopped spinach,
  thawed, squeeze all water out
1 small onion, chopped very fine
1 cup real bacon or bacon bits
12 flour tortillas (small) Or 6 12-inch
  tortillas

Mix all ingredients except tortillas. Spread mixture on tortillas and roll up. Refrigerate overnight. Before serving cut into 1" slices using a serrated-edge knife. Serves: 10-12

Genevieve Greenlee
Sacramento, CA

Tropical Quesadilla

Ron Fleming - 4th Street Grille

Chef/Owner of the 4th Street Grille. Ron cultivated his southwestern/Pacific Rim/California cooking style with chef stints in Arizona and as sous chef for the Hyatt chain in Sacramento and the prestigious Hyatt at Poipu on Kauai Hawaii.

2 flour tortillas
1/2 cup pepper jack cheese
1/4 cup goat cheese
5 ounces rock shrimp
2 green chiles

Salsa:
1 cup ripe papaya, diced
1 cup fresh pineapple, diced
2 tablespoon cilantro, chopped
2 tablespoon red bell pepper, diced
2 tablespoon red onion, diced
2 limes
1 lemon
Salt & Pepper

Heat griddle or saute pan. Brush tortillas with oil.

Place oil side down, then add jack and goat cheese to both sides.

Saute shrimp and diced chiles into middle of tortilla.

When cheese is melted put together and cut into wedges. Serves: 2.

For Salsa: Dice all ingredients and combine in bowl. Squeeze the juice from lemon and limes.

Add salt and pepper to taste.

Caviar Egg Ring

8 hard-boiled IGA California eggs
1 small onion, minced
1/4 teaspoon dry Schilling mustard
2 tablespoons lemon juice
1/4 teaspoon MSG (may be omitted)
1/2 cup Kraft mayonnaise
1/2 cup Crystal butter or Kraft
    margarine, melted but not hot
1 cup caviar
4 tablespoons snipped parsley

Bev Williams
Penn Valley, CA

Chop eggs. Mix onion, mustard, lemon juice and MSG. Add mayonnaise and margarine. Gently fold in eggs. Pour into oiled 1 quart ring mold. Chill for at least 5 hours.

To serve: Unmold carefully and fill center with caviar. Sprinkle with chopped parsley

Note: I normally pour egg salad in pie plate, chill and top with drained caviar, top with chopped green onions. Yields: 16

Fruit Dip

2 IGA California eggs
2 tablespoons corn starch
2 tablespoons water
1 cup orange juice
1 cup IGA sugar
juice of 2 lemons
1/2 cup Crystal cream, whipped

Karen Rasmussen

Cook and stir ingredients. Cool. Fold in whipped cream. Use with chunky fruit: bananas, strawberries, pineapple, apples, etc.

Hot Bean Dish

1 large can pork and beans
1 can kidney beans, drained
1 can lima beans, drained
1 cup chopped bacon
1 cup chopped onions
1/2 cup chopped green bell pepper.
1 medium jar pimiento, drained and
    chopped
1 cup IGA brown sugar
2 tablespoons Worcestershire sauce
1 small bottle of catsup
1 1/2 teaspoon prepared mustard

Martha M. Simpson
Sacramento, CA

Brown bacon and drain, brown Onions in bacon grease. Mix beans all together, add bacon, onions, and green bell peppers. Add all the other ingredients. Bake at 350° for 1 hour.

Crab Appetizers

Larry Mitchell

Larry Mitchell is the General Manager, Hewlett-Packard, Roseville Site. He has been married for 29 years to his wife, Denise. They have two sons, Bruce and Scott, daughter-in-law, Lisa, and grandson, Nicolas. Larry is a native Californian who loves the outdoors, especially fly fishing.

1/2 cup Crystal butter
1 jar cheese spread
1 1/2 teaspoon Kraft mayonnaise
1/2 teaspoon Schilling garlic salt
1/2 teaspoon seasoned salt
1 can (7-ounce) crab meat
6 English muffins

Let butter and cheese spread soften to room temperature. Mix together and add mayonnaise, garlic salt and crab meat. Spread mixture on English muffin halves. Broil 10 minutes or until they bubble.

* I prefer to toast the muffins before I spread on the crab mixture.

* After broiling, cut muffins into quarters for appetizers

Spicy Hot Chicken Wings

5-pound bag of party chicken wings
1 cup red wine vinegar
1/2 cup hot sauce
2 tablespoons spicy seasoning salt,
    Cajun or Creole seasoning
1 teaspoon Schilling garlic powder
1 teaspoon black pepper

Rochelle Clipper
Stockton, CA

Put all ingredients (in order of recipe) into large bowl or marinating container, mix very well. Let wings marinate 24 hours. Set oven at 400° put chicken on grill for 45 minutes. 350° if you do not want crispy wings and put in shallow pan in marinate juice for 45 minutes. Different types of seasoning can be used, like barbecue seasoning, mesquite seasoning in place of what is above. Serves: 20

Artichoke Dip

2 jars marinated artichoke b ottoms
1/4 cup Kraft mayonnaise
1/4 cup grated Kraft Parmesan
    cheese

Jane Patterson
Stockton, CA

Drain artichoke bottoms, reserving the liquid from one jar. Put artichoke bottoms in food processor. Process until chopped finely.

Add mayonnaise, cheese and 2 tablespoons of reserved liquid. Process until of dipping consistency. Add more of the reserved liquid, if needed.

Very good with chips and excellent for dipping artichoke leaves. Serves: 4-8.

Southwest Nachos

tortilla chips
chili or black beans
shredded Kraft mozzarella cheese
shredded Kraft cheddar cheese
salsa
Crystal sour cream
guacamole

Johanna M. Cunningham
Sacramento, CA

Use 9 1/2 x 11 glass baking dish. Layer ingredients starting with chips in any combination, usually 2 layers is perfect. If you are health conscious most of these ingredients can be found fat-free. Layer chips, chili, cheese, salsa, chips, etc. Bake at 350° for 20-25 minutes or until cheese melts. Or microwave for 10 minutes. Top with condiments and enjoy. Serves: 6-8

Shrimp Puffs

2 packages of crescent rolls
4 ounces Kraft cream cheese
2 ounces bleu cheese
32 frozen shrimp
oil for deep frying (butter-flavored)

Eleanor Lawrence
Stockton, CA

Mix softened blue cheese and cream cheeses and refrigerate until ready to use. Prepare shrimp according to package and refrigerate until ready to use (this can be done early in day or day before). If puffs are to wait longer than 30 minutes before cooking prepare puffs and put on cookie sheet lined with wax paper, cover with damp cloth, and refrigerate until ready to cook.

To prepare: Unfold 2 crescent rolls and roll out into 5" square with rolling pin covered with cheese cloth stocking (roll on cutting board). Cut into 4 equal squares. Place 1 shrimp in center of each square. Place 1 tablespoon cheese mixture on top of each shrimp. Fold all edges up and twist together like pig's tail. Shape and round the puffs. Place on cookie sheet and cover. Repeat with 2 more flattened rolls, etc. until completed.

To cook: Deep fry in 3" of hot oil in deep fryer at 350°-375° or sauce pan on medium-high setting, until golden brown. Lower puffs into hot oil on a slatted spoon and remove with same. Don't overload container, puffs should not touch while cooking. Remove to paper towels to drain briefly, serve immediately. Yields 32 puffs.

Bean Dip

1 large can refried beans
2 large avocados, mashed
1 pint Crystal sour cream
1 envelope taco seasoning
Kraft cheddar cheese, shredded

Layer beans, then avocados, then sour cream mixed with taco seasoning, then shredded cheese. Put in 9 x 13 inch pan. Serve with tortilla chips. To keep avocados from turning brown add a small amount of lemon juice.

Frances (McMillan) Ratzlaff
Winton, CA

Mary's Corn Stuff

2 4-ounce cans diced green chilies
1 16-ounce can creamed corn
1 16-ounce corn muffin mix
1 large onion diced fine
2 cup grated Kraft cheddar cheese
3 IGA California eggs, beaten
1/2 cup Crystal milk
1/4 cup Wesson oil

Mix eggs, milk, and oil. Add muffin mix, stir until moistened then add remaining ingredients and mix well. Bake in 10"x15" pan at 425° for 30 minutes. To reheat cut into small squares and reheat at 300° for 15 minutes. Can be served warm or at room temperature. Serves: 36

Mary Fluetsch
Stockton, CA

Spicy Sweet Potato Balls

Marilyn L Morris

President United Way of San Joaquin County; farm girl from Oregon; originator of the "Pie of the Month" auction item for The Rotary Club of Stockton.

Three pounds sweet potatoes, cooked and pared or two cans (17-18 ounces each) sweet potatoes, heated and drained.
2 tablespoons IGA brown sugar
2 tablespoons Crystal butter
1/2 teaspoons salt
1/2 teaspoon Schilling cinnamon
1/4 teaspoon Schilling nutmeg
1 IGA California egg
24 miniature marshmallows
1/2 cup graham cracker crumbs

Mash hot sweet potatoes. Add brown sugar, butter, salt, cinnamon and nutmeg.

Add egg and continue mashing until thoroughly combined. Chill if not firm.

Form mixture into balls, using 1/3 cup for each ball and placing three miniature marshmallows in center of each ball, if desired.

Dredge balls in graham cracker crumbs; place in baking pan and bake in hot oven (400°) 10-15 minutes.

Yields eight sweet potato balls.

If canned sweet potatoes in syrup are used, brown sugar may be omitted.

26

Marinated Shrimp

2 1/2 to 3 pounds shrimp

Sauce:
1 1/4 cup Wesson oil
3/4 cup white vinegar
1 1/2 teaspoons salt
2 1/2 teaspoons celery seeds
2 1/2 capers and juice
5 small onions, sliced
7-8 bay leaves
2 lemons sliced into rings with skins

Kay Lehr
Sacramento, CA

Arrange shrimp lemon and onion in layers. Mix sauce in large measuring cup adding oil and vinegar, bay leaves, capers and juice, celery seeds and salt. Pour over onions and lemons. Cover and put in refrigerator for 2 to 3 days.

Three-Way Salsa: Sweet, Spicy, Savory

Mike Dunne

The Sacramento Bee

Mike Dunne is the food editor and a restaurant critic of The Sacramento Bee. He joined The Bee as a feature writer in 1978, and since then has been writing food and wine features and columns. He lives in Sacramento.

4 ancho chile peppers
2 medium-size tomatoes
4 cloves garlic
1 medium-size sweet white onion
2 canned chipotle chiles en adobo
4-5 ounces Mexican chocolate
1/2 cup apple-cider vinegar
1/2 teaspoon freshly grated orange zest
1/2 teaspoon dried Mexican oregano
1/2 teaspoon cumin seeds
1/4 teaspoon salt
1/2 cup pepitas (pumpkin seeds), roasted and salted
1/2 teaspoon canela molida, Mexican cinnamon

In a heavy, dry skillet over medium heat, pan roast ancho chiles until they are brown and fragrant, 1 or 2 minutes. Be sure to not burn . Cool slightly, slit open, remove seeds; set aside. In same skillet, medium heat, pan roast tomatoes until they are soft and their skin is blackened and blistered. Put in blender. In same skillet, over medium heat, pan roast unpeeled garlic until brown and soft. Cool, then peel and add to blender.

Peel onion and slice into 1/4 inch rounds. In same skillet, over medium heat. Pan roast onion slices until they are brown and soft. Cool, then coarsely chop and add to blender. Coarsely chop chipotle chiles en adobo and add to blender. Melt chocolate In double boiler. In a small saucepan bring to boil vinegar. Add ancho chiles and reduce heat to simmer. Simmer until chiles soften, about 5 minutes.

Add melted chocolate to saucepan with vinegar and chiles. Stir until blend resembles a dark, hot cocoa. Set aside to cool slightly. Add orange zest to blender. In same dry skillet, but with the heat reduced to medium-low, pan roast cumin seeds until brown and fragrant, about 1 minute. Grind in mortar and add to blender. In same skillet, over medium-low heat, pan roast oregano until fragrant, about 1 minute. Add to blender.

Add salt, pepitas, chile/chocolate blend and canela molida to blender. Puree until smooth but thick. The salsa is splendid with chips, but experiment with it in varying portions and applications with grilled meats and seafood. Yields: 2 1/2 cups

27

Soups & Salads

Stuart's Broccoli Salad

Stuart Satow

Stuart Satow, News 10's Sports Director and Sports Anchor, joined KXTV in 1980. Originally from Munich, Germany, Satow was raised in Sacramento. Stuart anchors sports weeknights on Channel 10.

2 bunches of Broccoli (bite sized pieces) - blanched
12 strips bacon - crumbled
1 small red onion - chopped
1/2 cup raisins
1/2 cup sunflower seeds

Dressing:
1 cup Kraft mayonnaise
2 tablespoons white vinegar
1/4 cup IGA sugar

Mix dressing ingredients. Combine other ingredients. Pour on dressing and stir. Chill before serving. Serves: 6

Green Chile Chicken Soup/Stew

Dick Cable

I have been with KXTV for over 25 years. I developed a passion for the green chile New Mexico is famous for. It is not usually available outside the region. Here, I use fresh Anaheim chiles. I like it hot, so I keep some seeds. If canned green chiles or jalapeno peppers are used, the outcome is distinctly inferior.

4 tomatoes/chopped
5 or 6 boiling Idaho potatoes/quartered and sliced
1 large onion/chopped
4 or more garlic cloves, chopped
10-12 Anaheim chiles, roasted, peeled and chopped
    (remove seeds, ribs and stems. Retain some seeds to increase heat)
6-8 boneless, skinless chicken breast-halves, cut in strips and then cross-sliced into serving-size soup pieces
1 gallon chicken stock
olive oil
salt

In soup pot, add potatoes to chicken stock and bring to boil. At same time, saute chicken breasts and half the garlic in a little olive or other oil. When they change from pink to white remove from saute pan (I use a wok). Add a little more oil and saute the rest of the garlic, tomatoes, onion and chiles, stirring until well blended and onions are clarified.

Add the chicken and any residual juices to the saute pan and continue to stir together another couple of minutes. Then simply add to the stock and potatoes. Salt to taste and cook until potatoes are done. Ladle into bowls and enjoy.

Recipe is for a large pot of soup/stew, which gets even better after a day or two.

31

Shredded Chicken Salad

Harry C. Elliott, III

Over the past 40 years, Elliott Homes has built and sold more than 25,000 single family homes. Leading this home building company is Harry C. Elliott III, the son of company founder, H.C. Elliott. Upon his father's retirement in 1984, Harry became president of Elliott Homes, Inc. Harry and his wife, Debbie, have four children; Roxanne, Harry IV, Chelsea and Nicholas. He enjoys racquetball, boating, skiing and roller-blading.

2 large heads iceberg lettuce
3 large bunches cilantro
5 skinless, boneless chicken breasts
4 ounces Chinese bean threads
fresh ginger root
Schilling dry mustard
1 bunch of scallions
1 cup of soy sauce
1/2 cup teriyaki sauce
2 teaspoons of hot chili/sesame oil
Wesson oil

Chop or slice chicken into pieces 1/2"x1". Place in marinade for several hours.

Marinade: Chop ginger root (About a 1" piece) and 4 or 5 scallions into small pieces and combine with soy sauce and teriyaki sauce.

Combine 1 tablespoons of mustard with 1 teaspoon of water to make into a paste and add with chili/sesame oil to marinade.

Bean threads: Heat 2" of cooking oil in a hot wok (375°-400° depending on type of cooking oil.)

Bean threads are translucent very hard, string-like stuff wound up like petrified string.

Put a small amount into the hot oil and it crackles and puffs up to a crispy almost foam-like string.

Try a small amount at a time until you get the hang of it. Sometimes you need to turn the whole bunch over as it is cooking as the threads in the hottest part of the oil expand and thrust the upper part out of the oil.

Scoop into a bowl lined with paper towels and set aside. 4 ounces of bean threads should yield about one gallon of cooked expanded threads.

Clean and separate cilantro from the stems, and combine with cleaned iceberg lettuce in a large salad mixing bowl.

Cook the marinated chicken in small amounts with only a small of marinade with it in the wok at about 350°.

Place in a separate dish until all chicken is cooked.

Lower temperature of the wok to about 300° and warm the remaining marinade as a sauce to be used as a dressing on the salad if desired. It is hot but it is great.

Add chicken to salad and mix well.

Add bean threads to the salad last so they don't absorb the moisture of the chicken quickly and become soggy.

Show-Stopper Chicken Salad

1 large whole chicken breast
3/4 cup celery, diced
3/4 cup pine nuts
1/3 cup green onions, chopped
1/3 cup parsley, chopped
1/3 cup golden raisins, plumped,
  soak in hot water about 20
  minutes, drain
1 cup red delicious apples, diced,
  soak in juice of one lemon to
  prevent discoloration
1/4 cup mustard vinaigrette

Dressing:
1/2 cup Kraft mayonnaise (egg-less)
1/2 cup Crystal sour cream
dash Schilling curry
salt and pepper

Marilyn Bachik
Stockton, CA

Poach and cut up chicken. Mix all the ingredients together. Serve over a bed of salad greens. Serves: 4-6

Clam Chowder

1 large can chopped clams
  (51-ounce can)
1 large can whole baby clams
2 bottles clam juice
1 large bag hash brown potatoes
1 large white onion chopped small
2 bunches green onions chopped up
  to greens
1 quart Crystal half & half
1 1/2 sticks of Crystal butter
1 tablespoon salt
1/2 tablespoon Mrs. Dash
1 tablespoon fresh or dry Schilling
  parsley
1 medium shake of black pepper (to
  taste)
1 big shake of Schilling cayenne
  pepper
2 tablespoons flour

Ron and Lou Bruegger
Auburn, CA

Saute white onions in butter. Drain clams and set clams aside, add all clam juice to pot. Add all spices, green onions to pot, bring to a boil then add hash browns and cook about 5 minutes. Mix flour with 2/3 cup of water (shake in jar to mix) then slowly stir into boiling mix and cook for an additional 5 minutes. Turn off and let rest for 8 to 10 minutes. Add half & half, clams, and cook for 5 minutes at medium heat. (Do not allow to boil) Serve.

Paella

In medium saucepan, combine water, rice, bouillon, red pepper and saffron, 1/4 teaspoons salt. Bring to a boil and reduce heat. Cover with a tight fitting lid. Cook approximately 20 minutes. Remove from heat, let stand 5 minutes.

In a large bowl combine rice, chicken, shrimp, tomatoes, artichokes, peas and onions. Toss gently to mix. Pour vinaigrette over mixture and toss lightly to coat.

Saffron Vinaigrette:
1 /3 cup olive oil
1/3 cup Wesson vegetable oil
1/3 cup white wine vinegar
juice of a fresh lemon
3 cloves garlic, crushed
1/4 teaspoons saffron
2 tablespoons dijon mustard
2 to 3 tablespoons Kraft mayonnaise

Combine all ingredients in a food processor until well blended. Serves: 8

Bill Snyder - William Glen

Bill Snyder is co-owner of William Glen. The distinct subtlety of Saffron and a light vinaigrette enhance the flavors in this version of this traditional Spanish dish. Wonderful summer evening fare. Serve with warm, crusty French bread.

2 cups water
1 cup long grain white rice
2 tablespoons chicken bouillon
1/2 teaspoons ground red pepper
1/4 teaspoon saffron
2 cups cooked chicken, cubed
8 ounces cooked shrimp
2 medium tomatoes, cut into chunks
14-ounce jar artichokes, drained
    and cut up
1 cup frozen peas
1/4 cup chopped green onions
3/4 cup Saffron Vinaigrette

Mushroom Bisque

1 pound fresh mushrooms
1 quart chicken broth
1 medium onion, chopped
7 tablespoons Crystal butter
6 tablespoons flour
3 cups Crystal milk
1 cup Crystal heavy cream
1 teaspoon salt
white pepper
tobasco sauce
2 tablespoons sherry (optional)

Jill Raukko

Wash mushrooms and cut off stems. Slice six caps and reserve. Discard dried ends from stems. Grind and chop remaining caps and stems. Simmer covered in the broth with the onion for 30 minutes. Saute the reserved sliced caps in 1 tablespoon butter and reserve for garnish. Melt remaining butter in saucepan, add the flour and stir with wire whisk until blended.

Meanwhile, bring the milk to a boil and add all at once to the butter-flour mixture, stirring vigorously with the whisk until the sauce is thickened and smooth. Add the cream. Combine the mushroom broth mixture with the sauce and season to taste with salt, pepper, and tobasco sauce. Reheat and add sherry before serving. Garnish with sauteed sliced mushrooms.

Chicken Salad

1 1/2 cups chopped cooked
   chicken
2 stalks celery, chopped
1 tablespoon red onion, finely
   chopped
1 tablespoon lemon juice
1 hard cooked IGA California egg,
   chopped
5 tablespoons Kraft mayonnaise
2 tablespoons sweet pickle relish
2 teaspoons prepared mustard
1/8 teaspoon Schilling curry powder
1/8 teaspoon garlic, finely chopped
1/8 teaspoon pepper

Cristina Gutierrez
Sacramento, CA

Combine chicken, celery, red onion and lemon juice.
Stir in egg, mayonnaise, pickle relish and mustard,
curry powder, garlic, and pepper. Cover, chill at least 1
hour. Serve salad on lettuce leaves.

Chinese Salad

Salad:
1 head cabbage
6-8 green onions
1 pack ramen noodles, chicken
   flavored
1/4 cup Crystal butter
2 tablespoons sesame seeds
4 ounces slivered almond

Dressing:
1 tablespoon soy sauce
1/3 cup Wesson oil
1/4 teaspoons sesame oil
1/4 cup rice vinegar
1/3 cup IGA sugar
salt & pepper to taste

Stephany Emig
Sacramento, CA

Break up ramen noodles, brown on medium heat in a
frying pan with butter, seeds, almonds and ramen
seasoning. Cool. Chop cabbage, onions, into little
bite-sized salad pieces. Add ramen mixture, Toss. Mix
dressing ingredients shaking well, toss through salad.
Refrigerate 1 hour. Serves: 4

* Add boiled shredded chicken for Chinese Chicken
Salad.

Chinese Chicken Salad

Dennis Haworth

I have been practicing Interior Design in Sacramento for over 30 years. I have had my own design business for 20 years, Dennis Haworth FASID & Associates. This recipe is a great summer dinner by itself. Also great for weekends to take to the coast or to the beach. Will keep for days. I usually make a double batch when entertaining more than six people.

1/2 regular cabbage
1/2 red cabbage
4 large boned chicken breasts
1 bottle sesame seeds
1 package slivered almonds
2 packages ramen noodles

Dressing:
1 medium bottle seasoned gourmet rice wine vinegar
1 medium bottle sesame oil
2 seasoning packages from ramen noodles

Chop up cabbage into a bowl. Boil chicken breasts until done. Chop chicken into chunks. Toast Sesame seeds and slivered almonds under broiler until lightly brown. Mix cabbage, chicken, seeds and almonds. Crumble noodles into the cabbage mixture.

Dressing: Mix together rice wine vinegar and sesame oil. More vinegar than oil (to taste). Put the seasoning packages from ramen noodles in with the dressing and mix well. Toss into salad. (If you use 1 whole head of each cabbage then increase the noodles to 4 packages and increase the dressing and almonds to taste.

Portuguese Sopas

4 pounds boneless beef chuck roast
1 cup red wine
1/8 cup red wine vinegar
1 can (16-ounce) tomato sauce
2-3 sticks cinnamon
8-10 whole cloves
12 whole peppercorns
2-3 cans beef consomme
Schilling oregano, Schilling cumin, Schilling rosemary, garlic, Schilling onion powder, salt and pepper

Theresa M. Ungles
Sacramento, CA

Trim all visible fat from roast. Brown meat on all sides then put into crock pot. Combine all ingredients, pour over meat and make sure meat is completely covered. Oregano, cumin, rosemary, garlic and onion powder are to taste. Cook on high until meat breaks apart. To serve strain the juice. In a large bowl put slices of french bread, (day old is best) serve meat and juice over bread in bowls. If more liquid is needed to cover meat you can add either more tomato sauce or consomme. Cook on high 6-8 hours or until done. Crock pots differ on heat.

Portuguese sopas is appropriate for a heartland recipe. The Portuguese people have been a large part of California history and especially the Sacramento, Pocket Road area, farming a great majority of the land which has now been developed with homes and businesses. Some of the local churches still hold Holy Ghost Festivals where sopas are served as they have traditionally been served for many years. Serves: 4-6

Tomato Basil Brie

Junior League of Sacramento

The Junior League of Sacramento is an organization committed to promoting volunteerism and improving the community through the effective action and leadership of trained volunteers. Its purpose is exclusively educational and charitable. In its fifty-two years, the League has provided volunteer service and more than one million dollars to the community through projects involving health, education, the arts, children, and women's issues.

1 pound brie cheese, rind removed
1/2 cup packed fresh basil leaves
2 tablespoons pine nuts
1 tablespoon olive oil
1/2 teaspoon garlic salt
1/4 teaspoon white pepper
1/2 teaspoon minced onions
1/4 cup freshly grated Kraft Parmesan cheese
3 medium tomatoes, peeled, seeded, and diced
fresh basil leaves for garnish

Chill brie, split in half crosswise and set aside. Mince basil leaves in processor or blender. Brown pine nuts in olive oil. Add garlic salt, pepper and onions. Combine basil, Parmesan cheese and tomatoes with pine nut mixture until well blended. Place half of this mixture on bottom half of brie . Top with other brie half. Spread remaining tomato/basil mixture on top. Wrap lightly in plastic wrap. Chill up to 4 hours to allow blending of flavors. Serve at room temperature, garnished with whole basil leaves. Serve with crackers or thinly sliced baguette. Serves: 12

Minestrone Soup

2 pounds short ribs
1 cup dried beans (lima or garbanzo)
2 cups water
1 large onion, chopped
3 tablespoons fresh parsley
1 stalk celery, diced
2 cloves garlic, chopped
1/4 green pepper, chopped
1/2 pound spinach, torn
1 cup pasta, cooked
1/8 cup IGA sugar
1 tablespoon Schilling oregano
1 tablespoon Schilling basil
1 teaspoon Schilling thyme
6 peppercorns, diced
2 medium Idaho potatoes
2 cups tomatoes
1 cup shredded cabbage
1 small zucchini, thinly sliced

Mary Williams

Soak beans overnight, drain. Brown short ribs in large heavy pot. Add beans and cover with water. Simmer until tender (about 3 hours). Saute onion, parsley, celery, garlic and green pepper in olive oil until onion is translucent. Add all vegetables to meat and bring to boil. Then reduce heat and simmer for 30-45 minutes. Serve topped with Parmesan cheese.

Hazel's Shredded Chicken Salad

Jeff Morey - Hazel's Restaurant

Jeff Morey is the owner of Hazel's Elegant Dining, Modesto's premier 7-course continental restaurant. Age 42, raised in Los Angeles, degree in culinary arts, certified chef. He has been in the hospitality industry for 25 years, both in front and back of house operations. They will celebrate their 10th year in Modesto in 1995.

breast of Chicken, enough to give
    you six ounces of meat
3 tablespoons toasted sesame seed
2 ounces sliced toasted almonds
pepper and salt to taste
hot mustard to taste
6 sprigs of cilantro
3 green onion
1/4 head shredded lettuce
red leaf lettuce, enough to underline
    the plate
1 package rice sticks, prepared
    according to directions.
sesame/peanut dressing

Dressing:
22 ounces of sesame oil
22 ounces of peanut oil
1 jar of Chinese five spice.

Coat a bone-in, skin on chicken breast piece in a mixture of corn starch and water. Deep fry in 350° cottonseed oil until done. Peel the meat away from the bone and skin. Finely shred the chicken in strips by hand. Set aside.

Toast the sesame seeds and almonds in a saute pan until brown. Pick the cilantro leaves from the stems and set aside. Using only the last two inches of the green onion bulb, cut off the root.

Carefully slice the onion lengthwise so you have slivers when you are finished. Shred the lettuce very fine.

Add all ingredients except the rice sticks and toss thoroughly. Add sesame/peanut dressing to coat ingredients. Add the rice sticks (About three-four handfuls) and mix again. Taste and add seasoning as needed. Serve heaping on a red leaf underlined plate.

Place all ingredients in a shaker container and cover. Shake thoroughly. Continue to shake as you are pouring over the salad. Serves: 15

Tomalito Soup

Maria A. Padilla

Suzy's Mexican Food

1 bunch of spinach leaves rinsed
    and separated
2 cups corn flower (Masaharina)
1/3 cup lard
1 1/3 teaspoons salt
1 1/2 teaspoons baking powder
1 1/2 cups of chicken broth
3 pounds of pork butt (cut into 2 inch
    cubes)
15 tomalitos
3 Chiles De Arbol or small hot chiles
    such at Japones
4 garlic cloves

Dough: Mix lard until light and fluffy add masaharina, salt, baking powder, gradually add enough broth making a mushy dough. Add a teaspoon of dough on to the spinach leaf wrapping the dough like a taquito (tortilla roll) cook the Tomalitos in a steamer with about 2 1/2 cups water, at a low heat for 1 hour. Until tomalitos are firm.

Sauce: combine tomalitos, chiles, garlic and 2 cups of water in blender, set aside.

Pork: Place diced pork into a heavy casserole with sauce of the tomalitos and 2 cups of water more, and cook over low heat until pork is tender.

Serve 4 or 5 tomalitos into a medium deep plate add sauce and pork over tomalitos and enjoy.

Spicy Shrimp and Scallop Pasta Salad

Lina Y. Fat

California Fats Grill & Wok

Fat City

For Lina Fat, creating a new dish is part art, part science. She starts with inspiration. Then she analyzes similar dishes. Next, she imagines variations, and mentally tastes them. Only then does Lina actually begin to cook, balancing the Chinese standards of culinary propriety with the Western need for excitement and novelty.

Thai Dressing:
1/4 cup minced shallots
1 tablespoon minced fresh ginger
1 tablespoon chopped, fresh basil
1 tablespoon chopped cilantro
 (Chinese parsley)
6 tablespoons lime juice
1/4 cup Thai fish sauce
1 tablespoon IGA sugar
1/2 teaspoon salt
1/8 teaspoon crushed, dried red
 chiles
1/2 cup Wesson oil

8 dried Chinese black mushrooms
2 cups chicken broth
1/2 pound medium raw shrimp,
 shelled and deveined
1/2 pound sea scallops, quartered
1 pound tri-colored spiral-shaped
 pasta
1/4 cup roasted peanuts, coarsely
 chopped
cilantro (Chinese parsley) sprigs for
 garnish

This pasta salad tastes especially fresh and bright. The secret is the Thai dressing which contrasts sweet, sour, salty, and spicy flavors.

Prepare the dressing in a blender or food processor, whirl shallots, ginger, basil, cilantro, lime juice, fish sauce, sugar, salt, and chiles until smoothly blended.

With motor running, add oil in a slow stream.

Soak the mushrooms in warm water to cover for 30 minutes; drain. Cut off stems and cut caps in quarters.

Heat chicken broth to simmering in a 2-quart pan. Add mushrooms, shrimp and scallops.

Simmer until shrimp turn pink and scallops are barely tender, 2 to 3 minutes.

Drain; reserve poaching liquid for other uses.

Place shrimp mixture in a bowl, add 1/2 cup of Thai dressing, and stir to coat.

Refrigerate, covered, for at least 2 hours.

Cook pasta in a large kettle of boiling salted water according to package directions until barely tender to bite.

Drain, rinse with cold water, and drain again. In a large bowl toss pasta with shrimp mixture.

Add enough of the remaining dressing to coat pasta lightly; toss.

Place in a wide shallow serving bowl, sprinkle with peanuts, and garnish with cilantro.

Note: In Thai cooking, fish sauce, also called nam pla, is used the way Chinese cooks use soy sauce. It is lighter in color and less salty than soy sauce, and despite its name, it does not taste fishy. Look for it in Asian markets.

Serves: 6

Cucumber Salad

2 packages lime flavored gelatin (3
    ounces each)
1 1/2 cups hot water
12 ounces Kraft cream cheese
    softened
2 cups Kraft Miracle Whip
2 teaspoons prepared horseradish
1/2 teaspoon salt
4 tablespoons lemon juice
1 1/2 cups drained, shredded or
    ground pared cucumbers
1/4 cup finely cut green onion.

Terri Sasser
Stockton, CA.

Dissolve gelatin in hot water, add cheese, salad dressing, horseradish and salt. Beat with electric beater until smooth. Add lemon juice. Chill until partially set. Stir in drained cucumbers and onion. Need a 6 cup mold. Serves: 8

A Salad for All Seasons

Gloria Glyer

Gloria Glyer baked her first cake at about age 4 at the Surcease Mine, where her mother was camp cook and her father was the blacksmith. She's been cooking ever since, taking some time off to graduate from Grant Union High School, Sacramento City College and Sacramento State College. She writes and modems in a weekly column called Helping Others to The Sacramento Bee. She also is doing other free-lance writing and may even write the family cookbook, once she masters the computer.

1/3 to 1/2 cup chopped almonds,
    walnuts or pecans
1/3 cup fresh lemon juice
1/3 cup Wesson or olive oil
2 tablespoons poppy seeds
2 tablespoons honey and Dijon or
    whole-grain mustard
1/2 teaspoons grated lemon peel
1/2 cup moist-pack dried apricots
4 cups bite-sized cooked chicken or
    turkey
1 medium-size red apple
1/4 cup sliced green onion, includ-
    ing green tops
salt to taste
Romaine or butter lettuce leaves

Spread chopped nut meats in shallow baking pan and toast in a 350° oven until golden (about 8 minutes); set aside.

Combine lemon peel and juice with oil, poppy seeds, honey and mustard in medium size bowl. Add apricots and stir to coat; cover and let stand for 30 minutes to 1 hour (chop apricots if you prefer).

Lift out apricots and set aside (you may have to scrape the dressing off the apricots). Stir chicken or turkey into dressing.

Core and thinly slice apple. Stir apple, onions and nuts into mixture; season to taste with salt. Arrange lettuce on 4 plates; divide salad between plates and top each salad with apricots. Serve with toasted English muffins and iced tea.

Note: apricots and chicken mixture may be prepared a day in advance and refrigerated in separate containers; bring to room temperature before completing. Salad may be prepared several hours in advance. This is a true California salad with all ingredients, except maybe the poppy seeds, produced in the state.

The salad invites variations and additions: thinly sliced celery could be added; dried peaches may be substituted; fresh pineapple is a possibility, although it is not a California product. Do not vary the dressing, it is the key. Serves: 4 as an entree

Chipolte Chicken Salad

Roxanne O'Brien

First Immigrant Cafe

Roxanne O'Brien has been working in restaurants for 20 years. She is currently chef at First Immigrant Cafe where she also teaches cooking classes. Besides cooking (or food) her other passion is painting. Roxanne is a recognized artist represented by Michael Himovitz Gallery and has shown nationally and internationally.

8-5 ounce boneless, skinless chicken breasts
1/4 large red onion, diced
4 celery stalks, sliced
1/2 red bell pepper, diced
1 ear of corn
1/4 cup chopped cilantro
Romaine lettuce

Dressing:
1/2 cup mayonnaise
1/2 cup Crystal sour cream
2 canned chiles chipoltes, seeded and minced*
2 tablespoons lime juice
2 garlic cloves, minced
1 teaspoon ground Schilling cumin
1 teaspoon salt
Freshly ground pepper to taste

Garnish:
cherry tomato halves
lime wedges
cucumbers

Place chicken breasts on a parchment-lined baking sheet and cover with aluminum foil. Bake in a 350° preheated oven for 20 minutes. Let cool and tear in bite-size strips.

Scrape corn from ear with a sharp knife and blanch in simmering water for 2 minutes. Drain well and pat dry with a paper towel.

Combine chicken, onion, celery, pepper, corn and cilantro. Mix together ingredients for dressing. Add to chicken and vegetables and toss.

Line a platter with romaine leaves and shred some as a bed for the salad. Top with the chicken salad and garnish with cherry tomato halves, lime wedges and cucumbers. Serves: 8.

Additions:
1. Serve individual salads on a tortilla as a tostada.

2. Other salad additions or garnishes could include black beans, black olives, avocados, summer squash or radishes. In the summer it's nice to use fresh baby corn.

*Canned Chipolte Chiles En Adobo can be found in the Mexican food section of most grocery stores. Be careful when handling chiles, as they can burn eyes and skin.

Pasta Salad

16 ounces tri-color rotelle pasta
2 cups fresh broccoli chopped
1 cup carrots chopped
small can of sliced black olives
1/4 cup of cut up fresh parsley
1 Large bottle of Kraft Italian dressing
Kraft Parmesan cheese
pepper to taste

Cook pasta according to directions on package. Combine remaining ingredients and toss with pasta and dressing. Sprinkle Parmesan cheese on top. Chill, preferably overnight. Serves: 8

Dr. Ron Feist

Dr. Ron Feist is the Superintendent of the Eureka Elementary School District.

Bleu Cheese Dressing

2 cups buttermilk
1 quart Kraft mayonnaise
1 1/2 packages fresh bleu cheese
1/4 cup Schilling dried onion
3 tablespoons Schilling garlic salt

Blend all together, make sure bleu cheese is crumbled, let set 2 to 3 hours in refrigerator before serving. Use on salad, baked potatoes, potato chips and as a dip for fresh vegetables!

Bev Raty
Suisun, CA

Clam Chowder

Reverend David Bennett

Pastor of First United Methodist Church of Loomis. Member of Board of Directors of the Child Abuse Prevention Council of Placer County.

1/2 cube Crystal butter
3 cans clams
1 quart Crystal half & half
2-3 Idaho potatoes, diced
2-3 carrots, grated
1-2 stalks celery, diced
1/2 cup chopped onion
1 cup water
salt and pepper to taste

Bring to a boil the water, clams (with juice), potatoes, carrots, celery and onions. Turn heat to low. Add the half and half and butter. Simmer until cooked. Serve with lots of sourdough bread and enjoy! Serves: 4-6

Candy's Kitchen Soup

Candy Stevens

After getting her radio start in Oregon and Washington, Candy found her niche in the Central Valley. Nine years later she is currently hosting a morning show with Steve Jackson on Joy 99 FM. K J O Y 99.3. "I've been with K J O Y for five years now and enjoy it as much today as I did when I cracked the mike for the very first time". She currently resides in the country with an assortment of animals. "They know that when "mom's" in the kitchen there's sure to be a treat or two coming their way"

1/4 cup green split peas
1/4 cup yellow split peas
1/4 cup garbanzo beans
1/4 cup black-eyed peas
1/4 cup pink beans
1/4 cup red kidney beans
1/4 cup small white beans
1/4 cup large lima beans
1/4 cup barley
1/4 cup packaged 15 bean soup
1 large chopped onion
1 large ham hock (you may want to have your butcher cut into thirds)
2 tablespoons lemon juice
1 teaspoon Schilling chili powder
salt and pepper to taste

Soak first 10 ingredients in two quarts of water overnight. When ready to prepare soup, place soaked beans and peas in strainer and drain thoroughly. Then put into large pot with enough water to cover. Add ham hock pieces. Gently bring to a boil then simmer for 2 1/2 hours. Remove ham from hocks and discard bones, (I find my dogs to be willing helpers at this point). Ham stays in soup. Add onion, lemon juice, chili powder and salt and pepper to taste. Simmer 30 minutes longer. Enjoy!!

Serves: 8, Calories per serving: 190

Latitudes' Poppy Seed Dressing

Pat and Pete Enochs

Latitudes Restaurant

Pete and Pat Enochs' established The Kitchen, a folksy, vegetarian restaurant in Auburn, 16 years ago. In 1992 they founded "Latitudes," which quickly achieved recognition for the high quality of its service, ambience, and cuisine.

1 cup lemon juice
1/2 cup orange juice
1/2 cup water
1/4 cup honey
1 1/2 cup tahini
3 cloves garlic
2 rounds of red onion
1 teaspoon garlic granules (no salt)
1 tablespoon soy sauce
1/4 cup poppy seeds

We use an organic toasted sesame butter for our tahini. Keep your tahini refrigerated for a better product.

Add all ingredients except poppy seeds in blender in order listed. Blend well, until smooth. Add poppy seeds blend just until mixed, keeping poppy seeds whole. Containerize and store in refrigerator. Can keep up to 2 weeks. Shake to mix before using. Makes about 5 cups

Do not reprint without permission from Latitudes.

Sacramento Chicken Salad

Salad:
1 deli roasted chicken shredded
    (skin, fat, and bone removed)
8 cups shredded lettuce
1/2 cup fine 1-inch strips of bell
    pepper
1/4 cup coarse chopped cilantro

Dressing:
1/2 cup medium hot, fresh salsa
1/2 cup low salt soy sauce
1/4 cup Wesson oil

Garnish:
1/2 cup almonds, sliver, chop or toast

Norma S. Loeffler
Sacramento, CA

Place chicken, lettuce, tomato, pepper and cilantro in large chilled bowl. Mix well the salsa, soy sauce and oil. Immediately before serving, toss salad with dressing. Sprinkle with almonds. Serves: 4 as a main dish, Serves: 8-10 as a side dish

Chinese Chicken Salad

Congressman Robert T. Matsui

Robert Matsui was elected to Congress in 1978 and has gained a national and international reputation as a leader on far-reaching and complex public policy issues.

4 whole chicken breasts, skinned and boneless
olive oil
4 bunches watercress, cleaned with hard stems removed
1 bunch green onions, slivered
1 small red onion, sliced
salt and pepper
1/3 package won ton skins, slice in 1/4" strips, fry until
    golden brown

Dressing:
1/2 cup soy sauce
1/2 cup red wine vinegar
1/2 cup blended oil (olive, sesame, corn)
1 teaspoon IGA sugar
1 teaspoon hoisin sauce

Blend together all dressing ingredients. Brush chicken with olive oil and bake at 375° for 35 minutes. Slice baked chicken while hot into wide strips. Toss chicken with dressing in a bowl and set aside. (You may refrigerate the chicken and dressing until ready to use.)

When ready to serve, place watercress, green onions, red onion in a large salad bowl. Add drained chicken and toss. Additional dressing and salt & pepper may be added. Place fried won ton slices on top and toss.

Serves: 8 as a main course. This is especially good if served along with a wild rice salad and some fruit.

Wild Rice Salad

Susan Barry

4 ounces currants
2 tablespoons sherry
1 cup wild rice
1 cup Basmati rice
3 cups cooked chicken
grated zest of one orange
4 ounces dried apricots, sliced thinly
4 ounces lightly toasted pecans,
    chopped coarsely
one bunch chives, sliced

Dressing:
1/3 cup fresh lemon juice
1/4 cup fresh orange juice
1 tablespoon grated, fresh ginger
3/4 teaspoon salt
1/4 teaspoon black pepper
1/2 cup safflower oil
1/4 cup olive oil

Soak currants in the sherry. Cook wild rice and Basmati rice separately according to brand instructions, using salted water. Cool the rice. Add remaining salad ingredients and toss gently with dressing. Serve salad over a bed of mixed lettuces. For dressing: mix together lemon juice, orange juice, ginger, salt and pepper. Whisk in oils a little at a time. Serves: 8

Oriental Chicken Salad

1 package ramen noodles, chicken
    flavored
1/2 head cabbage
6 green onions, sliced thin
2 carrots, shredded
4 chicken breasts, boned and
    cooked
1/2 can sliced water chestnuts
1 cup almonds, sliced and roasted
2 tablespoons sesame seeds,
    roasted

Dressing:
1/3 cup Wesson oil
2 tablespoons IGA sugar
1/2 teaspoons salt
2 tablespoons rice vinegar
2 tablespoons water
1 package of chicken seasoning mix

Carol L. Thomas
Stockton, CA

Crumble noodles while still in the bag and then place in a bowl. Make salad dressing, pour over noodles, and distribute evenly. Microwave for 1 minute and let stand for 30 minutes. Shred cabbage and combine with onions and carrots. Cut chicken into bite size pieces and add to cabbage mixture. Add water chestnuts, almonds and sesame seeds. Mix well. Combine chicken mixture with noodles and stir to blend. Serves: 4-6

Bean Salad

2 1/2 cups red kidney beans
6 tablespoons crushed pineapple
1/3 cup pineapple juice
2 tablespoons coconut
5 tablespoons chopped almonds
1/2 cup Crystal cottage cheese
6 lettuce leaves
1/2 teaspoon Schilling nutmeg
1/2 teaspoon Schilling cinnamon
2 tablespoons Kraft cream cheese

Jeanette Ann Green
Modesto, CA

Mix ingredients except lettuce leaves, nutmeg, cinnamon and juice in medium size bowl. Place lettuce leaves in small serving bowls, serving about 4 to 6 and put bean mixture into lettuce leaves. Sprinkle nutmeg and cinnamon and add juice. Serves: 4-6

Menudo

10 pounds honey comb tripe
1 large onion
3 large cloves garlic
salt to taste
2 large cans hominy
2 packages pigs feet
1 bottle or 1 package chili powder
    (California Mild or New Mexico Hot).

Mercedes Garcia & Linda Lucero
Stockton, CA

Cut tripe into bite-sized pieces, wash and put in large pot with water. Cut onions into quarters, peel garlic, and add to pot. Bring to boil. After tripe comes to boil, turn down and let cook for 2 more hours, then add pigs feet. Cook until bones from pigs feet separate from meat. Add hominy, salt to taste. At this time add chili powder to desired taste. Cook 15 more minutes. Garnish with chopped onions, lemon, and oregano. Serve with corn or flour tortillas. Serves: 10 to 15

Pam's Chicken Salad

Pamela Gallagher

Gallaghers Place

Pam is owner of "Gallaghers Place" in Auburn. Pam has owned an Antique Business and a Bookstore since she and her husband, John, moved here 5 years ago. The present coffee, food and ice cream business evolved from the Bookstore.

1 chicken, de-boned
approximately 1 cup Kraft mayonnaise or to taste and
    consistency
1 cup celery to taste
1 can mandarin slices
1 can any style pineapple
1-2 apples diced
sprinkle Schilling curry to taste
sliced almonds or walnuts
salt and pepper

Boil chicken, remove and cool... shred chicken, place in bowl. Add all ingredients above. Mix well. At "Gallaghers" we serve it on a croissant. Serves: 10

Clam Chowder

Gary Counts

Bunz and Company

1/2 pound Crystal butter
1/2 pound flour
1 pound Idaho potatoes
1 onion
1 stalk celery
1/2 tablespoon Schilling thyme
pinch white pepper
2 16-ounce cans chopped clams
Crystal half and half

Rue: butter and flour, mix together

Add all other ingredients into pot with 1 1/2 gallons water. Bring to boil let boil until potatoes are done, thicken with Rue. When soup is thick, add half and half to thin down as desired. It may take all the Rue or you may have to make more. Soup should be very thick before adding half and half.

Tuna Salad

1/2 cup Kraft mayonnaise
1 can tuna drained
1 cup cooked peas
1/2 cup Schilling minced onion
2 tablespoons vinegar
4 ounces salad macaroni, cooked
1 cup chopped celery, dill weed
    and parsley
pepper to taste

Fran Knobloch
Burson, CA

Mix all together top with paprika, chill before serving.

Strawberry Pretzel Salad

1/2 to 2 cups pretzels
1/2 cup melted Kraft margarine
3 tablespoons IGA sugar
1 8-ounce Kraft cream cheese
1 8-ounce whipped topping
3/4 cup IGA sugar
2 small packages strawberry gelatin
2 cups boiling water
2 10-ounce packages frozen straw-
    berries, thawed

Lonnie MacDonald

Crush pretzels. Mix margarine and sugar. Mix together with pretzels and put into 9x13-inch pan. Bake at 350° for 7 minutes. Beat cream cheese until softened. Fold in whipped topping and sugar. Spread on cooled crust and refrigerate. Dissolve gelatin in water. Place in refrigerator to cool. Add strawberries.

Let gelatin mixture set in the refrigerator until slightly set and then spoon over filling. Refrigerate until set.

Creamy Corn Chowder

2 slices bacon, diced
1 small onion, thinly sliced
2 medium Idaho potatoes, pared
  and diced (2 cups)
1 1-pound can cream-style corn
1 1/2 cups Crystal milk (1 cup
  canned and 1/2 cup regular)
2 tablespoons Crystal butter
1 1/4 teaspoons salt
1/2 teaspoon IGA sugar
1/8 teaspoon pepper

Carolyn Chandler
Merced, CA

In medium saucepan saute' bacon and onion until golden. Add potatoes and 3/4 cup water. Bring to a boil. Boil gently, covered, until tender. Add corn, milk, butter, salt, sugar, and pepper. Simmer covered 5 minutes, until hot.

Mexican Shellfish Stew

1 quart chicken stock or canned
  chicken broth
2 cups canned clam broth or fresh
  fish stock
2 large dried quajillos peppers-or
  any chile, seeded
3 medium cloves garlic, peeled
1 8-ounce can tomatoes, drained
2 tablespoons olive oil
20 small clams, 1 1/2 pounds,
  scrubbed
3/4 pound medium shrimp-peeled
  and deveined
1 small onion-minced
2 tablespoons minced cilantro

Jeni Rose
Sacramento, CA

Shrimp and clams in a tomatoey broth with smoky (but mild) dried chiles. Use large dried chiles, such as chiles quajillos or New Mexico chiles, to spark this stew's broth base You can substitute one pound of any firm-fleshed fish, such as swordfish, tuna, or mahi mahi, for the shellfish.

Bring chicken stock and clam juice to boil in a soup kettle. Add the chiles; simmer until softened, about 10 minutes.

Drain the chiles, reserving the cooking liquid. Transfer the chiles and 1/3 cup cooking liquid to a food processor. Add garlic and tomatoes; process until smooth. Strain pureed chile mixture through a fine sieve, pressing on this puree to release its juice and pulp; discard the solids.

Heat olive oil in soup kettle. Add juice and pulp, cook over medium heat, stirring occasionally until this mixture is slightly thickened and amber colored, about 5 minutes. Add the reserved chile cooking liquid; bring to boil.

Add clams and shrimp; simmer until the clams open and the shrimp are opaque throughout, about 3 minutes. (Discard any clams that do not open.)

Ladle soup and a portion of the clams and the shrimp into each warm soup bowl. Sprinkle each bowl of stew with a portion of minced onions and cilantro; serve immediately. Serves: 4

Creamy Chicken Soup (with a twist)

2 cups Crystal milk
1/3 cup flaked or shredded sweet-
    ened coconut
2 Strips lemon peel (1/4 x 2 inches
    each)
1/4 cup Crystal butter or Kraft
    margarine
1/4 cup flour
1 tablespoon Schilling curry powder
1/2 cup plain yogurt
salt and pepper
about 1/3 cup each slivered al-
    monds and sliced green onions
    (including tops)

Chicken Stock:
5 pounds bony chicken pieces
12 cups water
2 carrots, cut into chunks
2 medium onions, quartered
2 stalks celery, cut in pieces (include
    leaves)
1 bay leaf
6 whole black peppercorns
1/4 teaspoon thyme leaves
2 sprigs parsley

Chicken:
1-pound chicken breast, split
1 cup celery leaves
1 large onion, sliced
4 whole cloves
3 cups Chicken Stock or regular
    strength canned chicken broth

Betty Field

Pre-pan Chicken and Stock; set each aside. In small pan, scald milk, remove from heat; add coconut and lemon peel, and let cool completely.

Pour through a wire strainer and discard coconut and peel. In a 3 quarts pan, melt margarine over medium heat.

Stir in flour and curry powder and cook until bubbly, gradually add stock and cook, stirring until thickened.

With a wire whisk, blend in coconut seasoned milk, yogurt, and chicken.

Season to taste with salt and pepper.

Heat until steaming.

Pass almonds and onions at the table to sprinkle over individual servings.

Chicken: In 3-quart pan, place chicken breast, celery leaves, onion and cloves.

Bring to boil over high heat; reduce heat, cover and simmer for 1 hour.

Lift out chicken and let cool.

Meanwhile, pour stock through a wire strainer set over a bowl; discard seasonings and vegetables and reserve stock. Discard bones and skin from cooled chicken; tear meat into bite size pieces.

In a 6-8 quart pan, combine chicken pieces, water, carrots, onions, celery, bay leaf, peppercorns, thyme, and parsley.

Bring to a boil over high heat; reduce heat, cover and simmer for 2 1/2-3 hours. Let cool.

Pour stock through a wire strainer and discard veg-etables, bones, and seasonings.

Cover and refrigerate for up to 4 days; lift off and discard fat before using or freezing.

To freeze, transfer stock to freezer containers, leaving about an inch for expansion at top.

Cover and freeze for up to 6 months. Makes about 12 cups. The delicate surprise taste in this soup, makes it one of my favorites. Serves: 6

Chinese Vegetable Soup

1 medium-sized onion, chopped
6-8 large cloves of garlic, peeled and halved
2 ounces dried Chinese black mushrooms
4-5 thin slices fresh ginger root
7 cups water
1 1/2 teaspoons salt
10-12 fresh mushrooms, cleaned and sliced
1 8-ounce can thinly sliced water chestnuts
2 tablespoons soy sauce
4-6 stalks of bok choy, stems and leaves separately chopped
1/2 pound firm tofu, cut in small cubes
1 cup fresh or frozen green peas
approximately 1/3 pound fresh snow peas
3-4 scallions, minced (keep whites and greens separate)
small amounts of rice vinegar and sesame oil, for drizzling on top (optional)

Henry Horn
Sacramento, CA

Combine onion, garlic, Chinese mushrooms, ginger, water and salt in saucepan or wok. Bring to a boil, partially cover and let simmer about 45 minutes. Strain broth and discard solids. (You may want to save Chinese mushrooms for a stir-fry) return broth to wok.

Add fresh mushrooms, water chestnuts, soy sauce, bok choy stems and tofu. Bring to boil again, lower heat and simmer, partially covered, 8-10 more minutes.

Heat gently 10-15 minutes before serving. When soup gets hot, add bok choy leaves, peas, snow peas and scallion whites. Following these additions, simmer just 5 minutes, then serve. Top each bowl with finely minced scallion greens and, if desired, light drizzle of rice vinegar and/or Chinese sesame oil. Serves: 4

Asparagus, Leek and Potato Soup

Leo French

Leo French founded Placer Title Company in 1973. He has been in the Title and Escrow Business for 35 years. He lives in Newcastle, CA, with his wife Eileen.

1/4 cup Crystal butter or Kraft margarine
1 large leek chopped (white part and 1-inch green part)
1 bay leaf
1/2 teaspoon Schilling thyme
6 cups chicken broth
1 1/2 pounds new red potatoes, quartered
1 pound asparagus, cut into 1" pieces
salt and pepper to taste

Melt butter in heavy sauce pan over low heat. Add leeks, thyme and bay leaf. Cover and cook about 10 minutes until leeks are soft. Mix in broth and potatoes. Bring to boil. Reduce heat and simmer until potatoes are tender, about 10 minutes. Add asparagus and simmer 5-8 minutes until tender. Discard bay leaf. Puree in blender in small batches. Add salt and pepper. Reheat and serve hot. Serves: 6-8

Light Italian Onion Soup

6 tablespoons Crystal butter
4 large yellow onions, chopped very fine
3 cups chicken broth
salt
freshly ground black pepper
large French bread croutons, fried in Crystal butter
grated gauyere and grated Kraft Parmesan cheese, mixed

Garnish:
chopped raw onion
chopped parsley

Loretta L. Canclini-Rubalcaba

Melt butter and add onion, then cover tightly and steam over low heat until pureed and soft. Add chicken broth and simmer for 15-20 minutes. Season to taste. Sprinkled fried croutons with cheeses and melt cheese under broiler. Put croutons in each soup plate and pour soup over them. Garnish.
Serves: 6

Sombrero Beef and Orange Salad

1 1/2 pounds beef top round, trimmed (about 1 1/2" thick)
3 oranges
1 mild red onion
1 head red leaf or butter lettuce
1/3 cup olive oil
1/4 cup balsamic or red wine vinegar
1 teaspoon IGA sugar
1/2 teaspoons salt and Schilling chili powder
1 large clove garlic, pressed
1 ripe avocado, thinly sliced lengthwise
12 extra large California ripe olives, sliced in half lengthwise
poppy seeds (optional garnish)

Marinade:
3 tablespoons each olive oil and fresh lemon juice
1 clove garlic, minced
1 tablespoon chopped fresh oregano or 1 teaspoon dried Schilling oregano
1/8 to 1/4 teaspoons Schilling cayenne pepper

Teresa Hannan Smith
Sacramento, CA

Place beef in shallow dish. Mix all marinade ingredients in bowl, blend well and pour over beef. Turn to coat all sides. Cover and let stand at room temperature while preparing salad ingredients, about 20 minutes.

Slice oranges into 1/4" thick slices, remove peel. Thinly slice onion, separating rings. Frame a large shallow bowl or platter with lettuce leaves. Arrange orange and onion slices in alternate rows, reserving room in center for beef slices. In shaker or screw-top jar mix the oil, vinegar, sugar, salt, chili powder and garlic.

Remove beef from marinade. Heat a large non-stick skillet on medium-high and cook beef 6-8 minutes per side, or until medium-rare. Remove beef, cool slightly; slice across the grain into 1/4" thick slices. Arrange on platter in center. Shake dressing and pour over beef, orange and onion slices. Refrigerate until ready to serve. Garnish with avocado and olive slices. Sprinkle lightly with poppy seeds, if desired.

Serves: 6; Preparation time: 25 minutes; Cooking time: 8 minutes

Breads

Mexican Corn Bread

1/2 cup Crystal butter or Kraft
    margarine
4 IGA California eggs, unbeaten
2 tablespoons IGA sugar
1 4-ounce can diced green chiles
1 small jar diced pimentos
1 #303 can whole kernel corn with
    liquid OR 1 #303 can cream corn
    (I prefer the whole)
1/4 cup diced onion OR 1 table-
    spoon instant minced onion
1/2 cup grated Kraft Monterey Jack
    cheese
1/2 cup grated Kraft sharp cheddar
    cheese
1/4 teaspoons salt
1 cup all-purpose flour
1 cup cornmeal
4 tablespoons baking powder

Louise Schnur
Auburn, CA

Cream butter and sugar. Add eggs, one at a time, mixing well. Add chiles, pimentos, onion, corn, cheese and salt. Mixing to blend well. Sift together the flour, cornmeal and baking powder. Add to other mixture, a little at a time, stirring until mixed. Pour into well greased pan or 10" iron skillet. (I prefer the skillet.) Bake at 400° for 1 hour.

Whole Wheat Bread

2 cups Crystal milk-scalded
1/2 cup Crystal butter-melted
2 teaspoons salt
3 IGA California eggs
1 cup cracked wheat
1/2 cup bran
1/2 cup honey
2 cups whole wheat flour
3-4 cups white flour
1 1/2 packages of dry yeast
1/4 cup warm water
1 teaspoon honey

Yvonne Sinclair
Rocklin, CA

Mix yeast, water and 1 teaspoon honey together and let set to soften the yeast. (Do not use metal utensils.)

Mix milk, butter, salt, honey and cracked wheat with enough white flour to make a soft "sponge."

Add yeast mixture (honey, water, and yeast) and stir until thoroughly mixed. Add eggs and mix thoroughly. Mix in white flour until the dough is not sticky.

Turn out onto floured board and knead (mixing in flour as needed to keep from being sticky) until bread feels like a "fat stomach" pushing back at you when you press. Place in a bowl with a tablespoons of oil in the bottom, roll bread over to coat top with oil.

Cover with moist cloth and let rise until size doubles, about two hours in a warm place (80°). Make into loaves and place in well greased loaf pans.

Cover and let rise until size doubles, usually about one hour. Bake at 375° for 45 minutes.

Turn out of pans to cool. Makes 2 loaves.

Fancy French Bread

1 cube Crystal butter (softened)
3/4 cup finely chopped green onions
3/4 cup finely chopped, fresh
 parsley
Sesame seeds
1 long loaf sour french bread

Denese Holden
Loomis, CA

Mix above ingredients until well blended. Spread on french bread loaves, cut in half lengthwise. Dot with mustard. Sprinkle with sesame seeds over top. Wrap each loaf half loosely in foil. Heat in 350 oven for 10-15 minutes. Cut in 2 inch wide pieces. Serve hot.

Tomato Bread

California Tomato Growers Association

1 envelope active dry yeast
1/2 cup very warm water (110°-120°)
1 1/2 cups skinned and chopped
 ripe tomatoes, or 1 1/2 cups
 canned plum tomatoes with some
 of their juice
2 tablespoons IGA sugar
2 tablespoons safflower oil
2 teaspoons salt
1 tablespoon fresh herbs, minced
 (combination of parsley, dill,
 oregano)
3 1/2 - 4 1/2 cups all-purpose flour
Softened Crystal butter or egg glaze
 for rolls

Note: Fresh tomatoes will provide less liquid, thus less flour is needed.

Puree the tomatoes. Blend the yeast, pureed tomatoes, sugar, oil, salt and herbs together, then stir in as much of the flour as can easily be absorbed.

Add enough flour until the dough starts to come clean from the sides of the bowl.

Turn onto a floured surface and begin to knead dough, adding as much flour as needed (takes about 4 to 6 minutes until you have a smooth dough). Put the dough into a greased bowl and turn so that dough is greased on top.

Cover with plastic wrap and let rise in draft-free, warm place until doubled in bulk, about 1 to 1 1/2 hours.

Punch the dough down and turn out onto a floured surface. Tear off 10 pieces the size of golf balls and form them into small rolls, pinching seams at the bottom.

Place 2 inches apart on a greased baking sheet. With the remaining dough, cut into 3 equal pieces. Roll into fat rolls and braid, pinching the ends together.

Place in a greased 8 inch bread pan. Cover rolls and loaf lightly with a towel and let rise until double in volume, about 30 to 40 minutes in a warm place.

Brush the rolls with softened butter or a beaten egg mixed with a teaspoon of water.

Bake both bread and rolls in a preheated 400° oven for 15 minutes, then remove the rolls and continue baking the loaf at 350° for another 25 minutes. Serve the rolls warm; cool bread on a rack. Makes 10 rolls and one 8-inch loaf.

Irish Soda Bread

2 cups flour (1/2 may be whole
   wheat flour)
1 teaspoon baking soda
1/2 teaspoon baking powder
1/2 cup IGA sugar
1/2 teaspoon salt
2 teaspoons caraway seeds
1 cup raisins
1 1/2 cups buttermilk

Deborah Lonergan
Davis, CA

Preheat oven to 350°, grease 9x5-inch loaf pan. Mix dry ingredients, add buttermilk and mix (batter will be thick). Bake in loaf pan 35-40 minutes until light brown. Great toasted! Makes 1 loaf.

Mystery Muffins

1 cup self rising flour
3 tablespoons Kraft mayonnaise
   (salad dressing will not do)
1/2 cup Crystal milk

Anne S. Glover
Modesto, CA

Combine above in a bowl, mix well. Put in 6 well greased muffin tins. Bake 425° for 15 to 20 minutes. Note: Mayonnaise contains oil and eggs. If plain flour used, ad 1 tablespoon baking powder. Yields: 6

Zucchini Oat Bread

2/3 cup applesauce
2 cups IGA sugar
4 large IGA California eggs (or 8
   whites if you're watching your
   cholesterol)
2/3 cup water
2 teaspoons vanilla
2 teaspoons baking soda
1 1/2 teaspoons salt
1 teaspoon Schilling cinnamon
1/2 teaspoon ground cloves
1/2 teaspoon baking powder
1 cup oats
3 cups shredded zucchini
2 1/3 cup flour

Debra A. Sampson Boogaard
Folsom, CA

Preheat oven to 350°. Combine applesauce, sugar and eggs in large mixing bowl. Slowly add the water until mixed well. Add flour, vanilla, baking soda, salt, cinnamon, cloves and baking powder and mix well. Stir in oats and zucchini.

Grease and flour 2 9x5x3-inch loaf pans. Divide batter evenly between the two pans and bake 60 - 70 minutes. (Rotate pans after 30 minutes to ensure even baking.) Cool in pans 10 minutes, loosen sides with a knife, and remove. Let cool completely before slicing. Slice each loaf into 12 slices.

Figazza

2 packages yeast
1 1/2 tablespoons IGA sugar
1 1/2 tablespoons salt
2 tablespoons olive oil
2 cups warm water (1/2 instant hot,
    1/2 cold)
4 cups flour

Joan Cortopassi
Stockton, CA

Combine yeast, sugar, salt, oil and water. Add flour. Put in warm place for 1 hour. Covered with a dish towel and hand towel.

Put lots of flour on board so that your dough will be workable.

Pour some olive oil in large baking pan and smooth out all over pan.

Put dough in prepared baking pan and push to edges. Cover with 1 cotton towel and 1 heavy nubby towel and place in oven for about one hour.

With floured fingers poke holes in Figazza

Pour olive oil in holes.

Bake at 425° until brown. 30-40 minutes.

Special Bunt Bread

frozen bread dough

Spread Ingredients (choice):
diced jalapeno peppers and Kraft
    Monterey Jack cheese
napalitos and cheese
coleslaw and grated cabbage
salsa (drained and blotted to
    remove excess liquid)
meat: chicken, turkey, ham, or
    leftovers (diced up)

Harold W. Dart
Sacramento, CA

Use frozen bread dough. Allow to thaw, roll out to one half inch thick. Spread base and choice of ingredients, roll up and set aside.

Lightly grease bundt pan with butter, margarine or Pam.

Sprinkle in poppy seeds, caraway seeds, grate almonds or other choice.

Place rolled bread in pan and allow to rise.

Bake according to directions or until lightly browned.

Invert over paper towels and allow to cool, serve inverted side up on serving dish.

Let your imagination go wild. Surprise your guests

Refrigerator Rolls

1 yeast cake
3 tablespoons warm water
2 IGA California eggs
1/2 cup IGA sugar
1/2 cup shortening
1 teaspoon salt
1 cup warm water
4 cups sifted flour

Millie Stiff
Loomis, CA

Dissolve yeast cake in 3 tablespoons warm water. Add mixture to eggs, sugar, shortening, salt and 1 cup warm water. Add flour and mix well.

Cover bowl and place in refrigerator overnight.

On lightly floured board roll dough 1/4" thick. Cut with floured 2" round cutter. Make a crease in center of each round. Fold in half. Place on ungreased cookie sheet about 1" apart.

Cover and let rise in a warm place — about 4 to 6 hours or until double. Bake at 450° for 5 minutes. Dough keeps 4 to 5 days.

Makes about 6 dozen.

Harvest Loaves

3 IGA California eggs
1 1/2 cups Wesson oil
2 cups chopped fruit or vegetables
1 1/2 cups IGA sugar
1 teaspoon vanilla
3 1/2 cups flour
2 teaspoons baking soda
1 teaspoon baking powder
1 teaspoon salt
2 teaspoons Schilling cinnamon
1/4 teaspoons cloves (or pumpkin
    pie seasoning)
1 cup of chopped nuts
1 cup raisins

Genevieve Greenlee
Sacramento, CA

Heat oven to 350°. Grease and flour 2 loaf pans.

Beat eggs, oil, fruit or vegetable, sugar and vanilla on low speed, scraping bowl often.

Add flour, baking soda, baking powder, salt, cinnamon and cloves and beat for 2 minutes on medium speed.

Stir in nuts and raisins. Spread in prepared pans. Bake 55-60 minutes or until wooden pick comes out clean.

Cool completely before slicing. Freezes well.

Variations:

Apple Loaves: 2 cups chopped, unpared apples;

Carrot Loaves: 2 cups shredded carrots, 2 tablespoons grated orange peel and 1 can (small) drained, crushed pineapple;

Zucchini Loaves: 2 cups chopped, unpared zucchini;

Rhubarb Loaves: 2 cups chopped rhubarb and 2 tablespoons grated lemon peel.

This recipe was from a cookbook printed around 1920.

Everything-In-It Eggnog Bread

2 cups all-purpose flour
1/4 teaspoons salt
1 cup IGA sugar
1 teaspoon Schilling cinnamon
1 tablespoon baking powder
1/2 teaspoon baking soda
1 teaspoon vanilla
1 1/2 cups eggnog
1/4 cup Crystal milk
1 IGA California egg
1/4 cup Wesson oil
1/2 cup nuts, your choice
1/2 cup raisins
1/2 cup candied fruit

Yvonne Carrie
Auburn, CA

In a large bowl combine all dry ingredients, then sift together once more and set aside.

In another bowl, combine liquid ingredients, plus egg, mixing until smooth.

Now mix in your nuts, raisins, and candied fruit.

Take set-aside dry ingredients and slowly blend into nut batter, again mixing until smooth.

Pour latter into a greased pan, (a typical, meatloaf-sized pan) lining bottom with wax paper.

Place in preheated 350° oven, and bake for about 1 hour, testing for doneness with a toothpick or knife.

Cool, then slice, serve. . .and watch it disappear!

Grandma Kelty's Banana Nut Bread

3 tablespoons Crystal butter
1 cup IGA sugar
1 IGA California egg
3 mashed Bananas (Ripe)
3 tablespoons Crystal milk
1 tablespoon Baking Powder
1/2 teaspoon salt
2 cups flour
1 cup nuts (optional)

Charlene Kelty
Auburn, CA

Grease loaf pan, preheat oven to 350°.
Cream together butter and sugar. Mix in egg, bananas, milk, baking powder, salt, flour, and nuts. Bake 1 hour.

Aunt Nan's Hominy Muffins

1 cup cooked hominy grits (cooled)
1/4 cup melted shortening
1 cup Crystal milk
1 cup flour
4 teaspoons baking powder
1 tablespoon IGA sugar
2 IGA California eggs, well beaten
1/2 teaspoon salt

Mix grits and milk in bowl. Stir in milk. Add flour gradually, stirring well. Add baking powder, sugar and salt, mix well. Spoon (3/4 full) into well greased muffin tins. Bake 350°, 25-30 minutes. Muffins will be soggy and best eaten with a fork. Yields: 12

Myra G. Burris
Modesto, CA

The "New" Banana Nut Bread

1/2 cup applesauce
1 cup IGA sugar
4 IGA California egg whites
3 ripe bananas (mashed)
2 cups whole wheat flour
1 teaspoon baking soda
1/2 teaspoon baking powder
1/2 teaspoon salt
1 teaspoon Schilling cinnamon
1/4 teaspoon Schilling nutmeg
1/2 teaspoon vanilla extract
1/2 -1 cup chopped nuts

Beat applesauce and sugar together. Add egg whites and banana pulp and beat well. Add sifted dry ingredients and vanilla. Mix well and stir in nuts. Pour into loaf pan (9x5x3-inch) that has been sprayed with cooking spray and floured. Bake in moderate oven (350°) for about 1 hour. Cool well and store overnight before cutting. Makes: 1 loaf

Brenda Cardwell
Stockton, CA

Potatoes,
Rice & Pasta

Puerto Rican Green Pidgeon Peas and Rice
(Arroz Con Gandules)

Geraldo Rivera

Geraldo is the owner of Investigative News Group, a company in association with Tribune Entertainment, which produces Geraldo's live specials, and the internationally syndicated daily talk show, Geraldo. This recipe originated from Hilda Rodriguez.

1 large can green pidgeon peas
3 cups of rice (small, medium or long grain)
1/4 Puerto Rican salami (salchichon) cut into 1/2" pieces
2 ounces tomato paste
1 large garlic clove (diced)
1 small onion (diced)
2 envelopes sazon
2 tablespoons Wesson oil
1 small pepper diced
8 small green olives
3 capers (alcaparrado)
3 cups water
a branch of coriander

Wash rice and place in a pot with water. In another pot simmer all the other ingredients, stir and let it cook about 5 minutes. Add to rice and let it cook at medium heat until all the water dries up. Stir, lower heat to low and cover. Cook for about 20 minutes stirring a couple of times. Serves: 5-6.

Balsamic Chicken and Pasta

1/2 each yellow & green peppers
1 whole sweet red pepper
3 tablespoons dried Schilling basil
3 green onions + part of chive
1/2 cup grated Kraft Parmesan
　　cheese
1/2 large onion
1 teaspoon garlic
2 carrots, grated
1/4 cup olive oil
3/4 pound angel hair pasta, cooked
　　by package directions

Marinade:
1/2 pound boneless, skinless,
　　chicken
1/4 cup soy sauce
1 teaspoon chopped garlic
3 tablespoons IGA brown sugar
4 tablespoons Balsamic vinegar

Bertha J. Duncan
La Grange, CA

Mix marinade in a medium-sized bowl. Wash & dry chicken, cut into strips or small pieces Add chicken to marinade - cover & refrigerate 1 1/2 hours.

Saute chicken in nonstick pan sprayed with Pam approximately 10 minutes. Set aside. Cut peppers & onion in strips, saute with: garlic and 1 tablespoon basil, leave slightly crunchy - toss with chicken

Saute grated carrots & sliced green onions with 1 tablespoon basil, add to chicken & peppers. Toss pasta with cheese and 1 tablespoon basil. When mixed, add chicken & vegetables. Drizzle with olive oil, toss well. Serves: 4 to 6, preparation time 30 minutes.

Bucatini all'Amatriciana Bianca
Bucatini with Pancetta, Hot Pepper and Pecorina

Biba Caggiano

Born and raised in Bologna, Italy's gastronomical capital, Biba Caggiano grew up eating and cooking the food of her native region. Biba is the chef-owner of BIBA restaurant in Sacramento. The restaurant has received glowing reviews from publications such as Gourmet Magazine, Bon Appetit, and Travel and Leisure. The January 1994 issue of "Conde' Nast Traveler" lists BIBA among the 200 best restaurants in the country.

4 tablespoons olive oil, preferably extra virgin olive oil
2 tablespoons butter
1/4 pound thickly sliced pancetta, cut into small strips
a pinch of hot chili pepper flakes
2 tablespoons freshly chopped parsley
1/4 cup freshly gated Pecorino Romano cheese or 1/3 cup Parmesan cheese
salt to taste
1 pound bucatini or spaghetti

Heat the oil and butter in a large skillet. When the butter foams, add the pancetta and chili pepper flakes. Cook gently, over medium heat until the pancetta is lightly golden, 2 to 3 minutes.

Bring a large pot of water to a boil. Add 1 tablespoon of salt and the bucatini. Cook, uncovered over high heat until the pasta is tender but still firm to the bite.

Scoop out 1/2 cup of the pasta cooking water and reserve. Strain the pasta and add it to the skillet. Stir in the reserved water, the parsley and 1/3 cup of Pecorino or Parmesan cheese.

Mix everything well over low heat. Taste and season with salt if necessary. (The pancetta is already quite salty.) Serve piping hot with a bit more cheese, if desired.

Tips - Pecorino Romano is a hard, sharp, salty cheese made from whole sheep milk. This cheese is easily available in this country in Italian markets and specialty stores.

When the sauce is comprised only of few tablespoons of oil, butter, hams, pancetto or vegetables, Italian housewives add a bit of starchy pasta water to the skillet, which in cooking down, thickens and moistens the pasta.

Fettuccine with Red Bell Pepper Sauce

Alan Frio

Alan Frio is the co-anchor of News 10 at 6 p.m. and News 10 at 11 p.m. He enjoys the great outdoors in his spare time. Alan is a runner and enjoys gardening. Almost all the vegetables he eats are homegrown in his garden!

2 tablespoons Crystal butter
2 tablespoons olive oil
2 1/4 cups roaster red bell peppers
2 cups chicken stock
1/4 teaspoon fresh ground pepper
salt to taste
3/4 pound fettuccine noodles
freshly grated Kraft Parmesan cheese
2 1/4 cups red onion
2 large cloves garlic

In large skillet, melt butter and oil, add onions, saute until slightly brown, about 4 minutes. Add garlic, saute another minute. Add peppers, stock and pepper. Cook 10 minutes. Transfer pepper mixture to food processor and puree. Add salt to taste. Cook pasta, spoon sauce over, sprinkle with parmesan. Serves: 6

Brown Rice

2 onions
1 1/2 cubes Crystal butter
2 cups rice
2 cans beef consomme

Freida Baskin

Brown rice and onions in butter. Add consomme and sliced mushrooms. Bake covered at 350° for 45 minutes to 1 hour.

Confetti Rice

Eddie and Marie Rishwain

Proprietor of Eddie's Carriage Trade Liquors and gourmet chef.

1/2 cup chopped onions
1/2 cup diced green pepper
6 tablespoons Crystal butter
10 medium size mushrooms sliced
3 cups cooked rice
1/2 teaspoon salt
1/4 teaspoon pepper
1/2 teaspoon fines herbs
2 tablespoons finely chopped parsley
2 tablespoons chopped pimento

Saute mushrooms. Lightly butter baking dish. (To make the nine cup ring mold double recipe.) Butter ring mold and line with buttered sliced almonds or pine nuts that have been browned in butter.

Saute onions and green pepper in butter until almost tender, and combine with remaining ingredients and put in prepared baking dish.

This can be kept in warm oven 10 to 15 minutes.

Brenda's Green Chili Potatoes

5 large Idaho baking potatoes
4 cloves fresh garlic, minced
1 1/2 cups Crystal sour cream
2 (7 ounce cans) chopped green
   chiles
1/2 pound cooked bacon, crumbled
2 cups shredded Kraft cheddar
   cheese
4 tablespoons Crystal butter
salt, pepper to taste
2 tablespoons Worchestershire sauce

Brenda Wilson
Sacramento, CA

Wash potatoes. Slice potatoes 1/4 inch thick leaving skin on. Layer half the potatoes in buttered 9x13-inch casserole dish. Top with sour cream, then green chiles crumbled bacon, cheese, then second layer of potatoes, salt, pepper, garlic, worchestershire sauce, and dot with butter. Cover with foil, Bake at 375° for 1 hour. This is great with meat or chicken. Great for parties and cookouts. Garnish with chives before serving. Serves: 6-8

Fried Rice

1/4 pound lean bacon
2 IGA California eggs
2 cups cooked rice
1/4 teaspoon each salt, pepper,
   Schilling garlic powder, Schilling
   onion powder
2 tablespoons Kraft margarine

Lety Acoba
Lathrop, CA

Cut bacon into tidbit size and brown. Pour off bacon drippings. Scramble eggs and fry in margarine in pan with bacon. When cooked, combine with rice. Season to taste with all other ingredients. Serve as main dish or with meat and vegetable.

Variation: Use hamburger or diced ham in place of bacon, use "egg beaters" in place of eggs.

Rice Torta

Dennis Haworth

This recipe is a favorite at our house on holidays.
An Italian Tradition.

2 cups rice
1 quart Crystal milk
1 tablespoon Crystal butter
1 bunch green onions
1/2 to 1/4 bunch parsley
1/4 cup olive oil
1 1/2 - 2 cups grated cheese
salt and pepper to taste
4-5 beaten IGA California eggs

Steam the rice, milk and butter. Let cool. Saute green onions and parsley in olive oil. Add steamed rice to sauted onions and parsley, cool. Add grated cheese, salt & pepper, and eggs. Mix well and pour into greased baking dish. Beat 1 egg and pour on top, spread evenly for browning. Bake at 350 until golden brown on top. Serves: 4-6

Tortellini Ai Formaggi

Giancarlo Bomparola

Il Fornaio

Giancarlo Bomparola is a third generation restaurants from a Milanese family. He began in his brothers restaurant cooking and managing the floor. He has worked in both capa cities in Paris, New York, San Diego and Palo A. Currently manager of Il Fornaio.

1 cup Crystal whipping cream
1/2 bouillon cube
1/2 teaspoon freshly ground nutmeg
pinch of white pepper
1 teaspoon Gorgonzola cheese
1/3 cup water
1/4 cup chopped basil
9 ounces spinach three cheese
    tortellini
1/4 cup grated Kraft Parmesan
    cheese

In a medium size pot, bring water to a rolling boil, adding 1 tablespoon of salt as the water begins to boil.

Meanwhile, in a medium skillet, heat whipping cream and bouillon cube. Stir continuously on medium heat, mashing the bouillon cube with the back of a wooden spoon.

Grate fresh nutmeg and add white pepper. The cream sauce will still be quite liquidy. Continue stirring and add Gorgonzola cheese.

hen add water and turn the heat up so the water evaporates. Sprinkle chopped basil and add to cream sauce shortly before pasta is to be added.

When the pasta is a couple of minutes from being cooked, drain and add to the cream sauce.

Toss to blend and lower heat to allow pasta to absorb the sauce.

Sprinkle grated Parmesan cheese and continue to toss pasta. After three or four minutes, the sauce will thicken.

Pasta is then ready to serve. Serves: 4

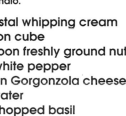

Mexican Rice

Larry D. Kelley

Larry D. Kelley, 48, is President of The Stanford Ranch Company. Kelley is a board member of the Placer County Child Abuse Prevention Council and a member of the President's Advisory Committee of California State University of Sacramento.

3 tablespoons bacon drippings
1 cup uncooked rice
1 medium onion, chopped
1/2 cup raw minced carrots
1 1/2 cups canned tomatoes
2 garlic cloves, minced
1 teaspoon Schilling cumin
1 can beef broth
salt and pepper to taste
several tablespoons frozen green peas for color
1 teaspoon or more of Schilling chili powder
3 tablespoons green pepper, minced

Heat drippings in large skillet. Add rice and brown. Add remaining ingredients, cover, reduce heat and cook until liquid is absorbed, about 25 minutes.

Caprock Chicken Spaghetti

1 (10-ounce) can cream of mushroom soup
1 (10-ounce) can cream of celery
  soup
1 (10-ounce) can cream of chicken
  soup
1 (10-ounce) can cheddar cheese
  soup
1/3 cup chopped bell pepper
1/4 cup chopped onion
1 (2-ounce) jar chopped pimento
1 (2-ounce) can mushrooms
2 ounces Kraft sharp cheddar
  cheese, shredded
salt and pepper to taste
3 pounds chicken, cooked, boned
  and chopped
8 ounces spaghetti, cooked
1/2 cup grated Kraft Parmesan
  cheese
1 (2-ounce) package sliced almonds

Myra G. Burris
Modesto, CA

Combine soups, green pepper, onion, pimento, mushrooms and cheddar cheese in saucepan. Cook over low heat for 30 minutes, stirring frequently. Add salt, pepper and chicken. Cook until heated through. Stir in cooked spaghetti. Spoon into greased 9x13-inch baking dish. Sprinkle with half Parmesan cheese, almonds and remainder of cheese. Bake at 350° for 30 minutes or until hot and bubbly. Serves: 10

Mama's Heavenly Macaroni & Cheese

Parnell M. Lovelace, Jr.

Pastor Parnell M. Lovelace, Jr. serves as the Founder and Senior Pastor/Teacher of the Center of Praise Ministries, Inc. located in Rancho Cordova, CA. He holds degrees in Human Services and Counseling, Social Work, and Social Services. Pastor Parnell has served in numerous community, health and social service programs.

5 cups uncooked macaroni
2 cups Kraft sharp cheddar cheese, shredded
2 cups Kraft medium cheddar cheese, shredded
1 can (13 ounces) evaporated milk
1 1/2 cups homogenized Crystal milk
5 IGA California eggs, beaten
1/4 teaspoon salt
1/2 teaspoon black pepper, ground
1-1/2 tablespoons IGA sugar
2 sticks Crystal butter

Bring 4 quarts water to a boil. Add macaroni and boil 8-10 minutes, or until tender. Rinse. Add butter to hot macaroni. Mix sugar, pepper, salt, evaporated milk, homogenized milk, beaten eggs together. Add to macaroni.

Add cheeses to mixture last. Preheat oven to 375°. Bake in large 3-4 quart pan or casserole until brown on top. Serves: 12 to 16.

Artichoke Linguini

Judge Rolleen McIlwrath

Judge McIlwrath is a Stockton Municipal Court Judge.

1/2 stick Crystal butter
1/4 cup olive oil
1 tablespoon flour
1 can chicken broth
1 clove garlic, minced
2-3 teaspoons fresh lemon juice
salt and white pepper (a tad)
1 tablespoon minced parsley
1 14-ounce can artichoke hearts
    (drain and slice)
2 tablespoons Kraft Parmesan
    cheese, grated
2 teaspoons capers, rinsed and
    drained
1 tablespoon Crystal butter
2 tablespoons olive oil
1 tablespoon Kraft Parmesan cheese
1/4 teaspoon salt
1 pound linguini, cooked
2 ounces minced proscuitto ham (or
    other ham)
garnish: 1/2 cup pine nuts

Melt butter with oil in sauce pan over medium heat. Add flour, stir until smooth for about 3 minutes. Blend in broth, stirring until thickened, about 1 minute.

Reduce heat to low. Add garlic, parsley, lemon juice, salt and pepper and cook about 5 minutes stirring constantly. Blend in artichoke, cheese and capers. Cover mixture and simmer about 8 minutes.

Melt remaining butter in large pot over medium heat. Stir in remaining cheese, oil and salt. Add cooked linguini and toss slightly. Place pasta on platter and top with sauce. Garnish with proscuitto ham. (Can make sauce ahead, keeps well.) Serves: 4

Just What The Doctor Ordered

1 cup white rice
1/3 cup wild rice
1 cup brown rice
4 2/3 cups water
1/2 -1 cup slivered almonds (pan
    toasted)
1-2 bags (8-ounce) of chopped
    mixed vegetables for salads
1/2 -1 cup cheese flavored salad
    dressing, low fat or regular
1 1/2 to 1 teaspoon black pepper
1/4 cup bottled lemon juice
Optional, if you want to get fancy:
Add;
chopped green onions, sliced
    celery, chopped green peppers
    and canned white chicken meat.

Ralph Koldinger, MD
Sacramento, CA

Put the three rices and water in a pressure cooker. Bring to full steam, then remove and let cool for 15 minutes. Toast the almonds. Empty everything into a big bowl and mix. Serve hot or cold on a nest of mixed greens. Garnish with canned sliced beets or quartered fresh tomatoes. Serves: 4-8

Pasta E. Fagioli

Steve Campanelli - Andiamo

His family's traditional Italian recipes have greatly influenced Steve Campanelli, executive chef at Sacramento's Andiamo Restaurant. Pasta Fagioli, a hearty yet healthy pasta with beans, is Campanelli's version of his mother's Sicilian recipe. This recipe is low fat and vegetarian.

1 can (15-ounce) cannellini beans, drained and rinsed
1/2 pound pasta, rigatoni or penne
3 tablespoons olive oil
bunch green Swiss chard, washed, stemmed, and cut into squares (or substitute frozen)
3 cloves minced garlic
1 sliced small onion
1 stalk sliced celery
1/2 teaspoon crushed red peppers
1 can (28-ounce) diced tomatoes in juice
1 teaspoon Schilling oregano
2 tablespoons chopped, fresh parsley
salt and pepper to taste
Romano cheese

Heat the oil in a large saucepan. Saute garlic, onions, celery, and red pepper for 2-3 minutes. Then add tomatoes and oregano and simmer about 5 minutes. Add beans, chard, and parsley. Simmer for an additional 4 minutes. Meanwhile cook pasta, then add to the mixture. Taste for salt and pepper. Top with freshly grated Romano cheese, and serve. Serves: 4-5

Options: Add 1/4 cup julienned strips of prosciutto ham; Substitute fresh spinach for Swiss chard; Use ditalini (salad macaroni) or other small pasta, thin with water or chicken broth if desired, and serve as a hearty soup

Sutter Basin Sweet Rice

1 cup uncooked California medium grain white rice
1/2 cup California raisins
1 1/2 cinnamon sticks
1/4 cup IGA sugar
1 tablespoon grated, fresh ginger root
3/4 cup IGA sugar
1 1/2 cups evaporated skim milk
1 1/2 cups non-fat Crystal milk
1 tablespoon powdered butter-flavor mix
1/2 teaspoon vanilla
1 teaspoon coconut flavoring

Richard & Sandra Giusti
Robbins, CA

Soak rice and raisins in water for 1/2 hour. Drain and add to 2 cups boiling water along with cinnamon sticks and sugar. Cook until rice is tender. Boil ginger root in 1/2 cup water 5 minutes. Strain this liquid into the rice along with sugar, evaporated skim milk, nonfat milk and butter-flavor mix.

Cover and cook over low heat until milk is almost absorbed, stirring every 5 minutes. Remove from heat and add vanilla and coconut flavoring. Spoon into serving dishes and serve at room temperature or chilled. Serves: 8-10

Wan's Pud Thai Noodles with Shrimp

Wan Binmahmood

Thai Palms Restaurant

Wan, of Thai Palms Restaurant, uses her extensive international travel, study and work experience (especially with the World Bank) to heighten her basic Thai cuisine in the creation of delicacies from all over Asia and the world.

1 pound dry rice noodles from Thailand (Chanthaburi noodles)
1 pound medium-sized shrimp, shelled and deveined
1/4 cup Wesson oil
1 tablespoon minced garlic
3 IGA California eggs
4 tablespoons Thai fish sauce (bottles available in most Asian markets.)
3 1/2 tablespoons white vinegar
4 tablespoons IGA brown sugar
2 teaspoons Schilling paprika
1 teaspoon ground dry chili peppers (or more, depending on spiciness desired)
1 tablespoon diced pickled radish (packages at most Asian markets)
1 1/4 pounds bean sprouts
4 ounces chives, cut to 1 inch
5 tablespoons unsalted roasted peanuts, coarsely ground
2 tablespoons green onions, chopped

Soak 1 pound dry noodles in cold water for 30 minutes and drain.

Peel and devein 1 pound shrimp. Peel and mince cloves of garlic to make 1 tablespoon. Wash 1 1/4 pounds bean sprouts in cold water and drain.

Remove the tails on 1/4 pound of washed bean sprouts for garnishing (save 1 pound for cooking).

Chop green onions to make about 2 tablespoons Coarsely grind peanuts to make 5 tablespoons.

Cut about 3 ounces chives into 1 inch pieces to make 1/4 c; cut about 1 ounce chives into 3 inch pieces for garnish.

Put 4 tablespoons of fish sauce and 3 1/2 tablespoon vinegar into small bowl.

Put 4 tablespoons of sugar, 2 teaspoons of paprika, 1 teaspoon of ground dry chili pepper and 1 tablespoon pickled radish into a small bowl. Turn large burner on stove to high heat.

Heat wok of about 18 inches diameter on the stove. Put 1/4 cup vegetable oil into wok.

When oil is medium hot, stir 1 tablespoon minced garlic into oil until lightly brown. Break 3 eggs into oil and stir with minced garlic.

Before eggs are cooked, add in rapid succession: 1 pound cleaned shrimp; 1 pound drained noodles; contents of bowl with fish sauce and vinegar mixture; contents of bowl with sugar, paprika, chili pepper and pickle radish mixture.

Continuously stir-fry by mixing all ingredients until the noodles are almost dry—about 2 minutes. Add 1 pound bean sprouts and 1/4 cup chives.

Continue stir-frying until bean sprouts are almost cooked — about 2 minutes.

Remove from heat. Remove ingredients from the wok onto a serving plate.

Sprinkle 5 tablespoons of ground peanuts evenly over noodles. Top with 2 tablespoons of chopped green onions.

Garnish with 1/4 pound fresh trimmed bean sprouts and 1 ounce of 3 inch long chives. Serves: 4

Crawfish Fettuccini

1/2 stick Kraft margarine
4 tablespoons olive oil
6 slices bacon, cooked, but not
    crisp, and cut up
1 whole large onion, chopped
3 minced garlic
2 cups chopped zucchini
2 cups chopped yellow squash
Schilling basil
Schilling thyme
white pepper
1 cup fresh chopped tomatoes
1 pound cooked crawfish tails, (may
    substitute shrimp)
2 teaspoons Creole seasoning
1 pound prepared fettuccine
Kraft Parmesan cheese

Mary Ellen King
Manteca, CA

Saute cooked bacon in olive oil and margarine. Add onion and saute with garlic. Add zucchini and yellow squash, saute. Add basil, thyme and white pepper to taste. Add the chopped tomatoes, crawfish and the seasoning. Serve over the fettuccini which has been tossed with olive oil and Parmesan cheese.

Blue-Ribbon Spaghetti Sauce

Daniel Kennedy

Publisher of the Sacramento Business Journal, and KXTV correspondent for the Business Journal segment on the 11 p.m. newscast. An avid gardener and tomato connoisseur, he resides in Davis with his wife and their children.

12 tablespoons olive oil
6 cloves garlic, chopped fine
2 medium onions chopped
1/2 gallon peeled, chopped fresh garden tomatoes
    (without skins)
2 6-ounce cans tomato paste
2 cups dry red wine
2 tablespoons each of dried Schilling basil and Schilling
    oregano (double if fresh)
2 teaspoons IGA sugar
2 tablespoons grated carrot (optional)
salt, freshly ground pepper to taste
2 29-ounce cans of chopped Italian plum tomatoes (if
    tomatoes are out of season)

Heat oil over medium heat, saute garlic, onion until golden: add tomatoes, tomato paste, red wine, herbs, sugar, and carrots. Simmer 1 1/2 hours. Add salt and pepper to taste. Freezes well for year-round use of abundant garden tomatoes. Serves: 12

Brazilian Rice

3 cups brown or white rice (cooked)
1 package cooked chopped
    spinach
1 pound ground beef, browned and
    drained
3 cups grated Kraft cheddar cheese
1/2 onion diced
1 clove garlic, minced
4 IGA California eggs
1 cup Crystal milk
1 1/2 teaspoons poultry seasoning
2 tablespoons A-1 sauce
1 tablespoon Worchestershire sauce
Kraft Parmesan cheese

Catherine Foley
Sacramento, CA

Mix all ingredient in a bowl except Parmesan cheese. Coat an oven bowl with oil spray. Pour mixture into bowl. Top generously with Parmesan cheese.

Bake for 1 hour in 350° oven or until inserted knife comes out clean. Children will eat their spinach when you serve this recipe! This can be served without meat for vegetarians, just omit the meat. When you omit the meat in this recipe, it can be used as a side dish. 6 large servings

This recipe can be frozen, I recommend dividing it in half when you do that.
* Monterey Jack and cheddar mixed may be substituted for plain cheddar.

Crab-Stuffed Potatoes

4 Idaho baking potatoes
1/2 cup Crystal butter
1/2 cup light Crystal cream
1/2 teaspoon salt
4 tablespoons grated onion
1 cup sharp cheese (grated)
5-ounces crab meat
pepper to taste

Cathy Contreras
Stockton, CA

Bake potatoes at 350° for 1 hour, until tender. Cut potatoes in half lengthwise; scoop out potatoes and whip with remaining ingredients. Refill shells and reheat at 425° for 15 minutes. Serves: 4-6

Cheese Potato Casserole

4 pounds frozen hash browns
1 cup melted Kraft margarine
2 teaspoons salt
1 teaspoon pepper
1 can cream of celery soup
1 can cheddar cheese soup
1 small onion (chopped)
24 ounce Crystal sour cream
1 1/2 cups Kraft sharp cheddar
    cheese (grated)
1 bag of potato chips

Robin Keen
Lodi, CA

Mix all ingredients. Bake at 350° for 1 1/2 hours. Top with crushed potato chips and bake for 15 minutes. Serves: 12-15

Spicy Curried Potatoes

Janet Lawrence Self

Janet is currently Regional Executive for United Way Placer County. She has 20 years experience working with non-profits and community development projects, locally and internationally. The recipe comes from her passion for international and spicy!

2-3 tablespoons Wesson oil
1 teaspoon mustard seeds
2-3 cloves garlic
2 inches fresh ginger
2 tablespoons Schilling curry
1/4 teaspoon Schilling cinnamon
1 teaspoon salt
6-8 large Idaho potatoes (scrubbed and diced).

Boil potatoes 5-8 minutes (Until just slightly soft) Drain and hold. In large frying pan, lightly fry mustard seed (they will pop, so have a lid). Add finely chopped garlic and ginger. Add salt and spices and fry for 2 minutes. Add drained potatoes and continue cooking until tender and potatoes are generously cooked. A cup of peas can also add a nice variation. Serve with plain yogurt on the side.

If you like it spicy, add 2 tablespoons crushed red peppers and a generous squeeze of lemon, just as you are ready to serve. Serves: 4-6

Heavenly Angel Hair Pasta

1 package angel hair pasta
1 package pesto sauce
1 pound sliced mushrooms
1/2 medium red bell pepper
3 cups broccoli tops
6 ounces crumbled Feta cheese
2 tablespoons olive oil

Kathy Miller
Loomis, CA

Slice bell pepper into 1-inch pieces. Break broccoli tops into small pieces. Saute broccoli, mushrooms, and red pepper until tender crisp. Stir in feta cheese. Prepare pasta according to package directions. Drain, then add to vegetables/cheese mixture. Serve and enjoy.

Parsley & Garlic New Red Potatoes

Charles Miller

Charles Miller is the co-owner/partner of the Michael Himovitz Gallery and is president of Professional Astrologers, Inc., a nonprofit, international business league. He loves good food and is fascinated by life and how the world turns. This is a fast and easy dish to prepare, delicious to eat and a great compliment to chicken entrees.

3 cups dices new red potatoes
1 diced elephant garlic clove
2 cups sliced mushrooms
chopped chives
chopped parsley
1/4 cup Crystal sour cream
lemon juice (preferably from fresh lemon half)
olive oil
Schilling herb pepper

While steaming potatoes, saute garlic, chives and mushrooms in olive oil. Add herb pepper to taste. Add steamed potatoes to sauted ingredients in skillet. Fold in sour cream. Add lemon juice and chopped parsley. Serves: 6

Rice Pilaf

1 cube Kraft margarine
1 heaping teaspoon instant onion
1 cup long grain rice

Dr. & Mrs. Robert G. Malone
Sacramento, CA

Saute this mixture at low temperature for 25 minutes stirring occasionally. (Best in heavy frying pan.) Place in casserole dish, add 1 can beef consomme soup, 3/4 cup of water.

Bake 40 minutes at 400° covered , or until all liquid has disappeared, and a brown circle forms around the edge. Serve with diced, toasted almonds on each individual serving. If you must wait on dinner, just turn down to warm, holds well in oven.

Steve Jackson's Killer Pasta Sauce

Steve Jackson

The voice of Steve Jackson has been heard on California radios for the last 23 years, currently mornings with Candy Stevens on KJOY 99.3 FM. Among the stations Steve has on his resume, 105.1 KNCI, KRAK FM 98.5, Y-92 KGBY, KNEW/KSAN, KFMR, and KO-93.

1 pound ground turkey
1 pound turkey Italian sausage
1 large yellow onion diced
1 large bell pepper diced
2 cloves garlic
1/2 pound sliced mushrooms
2 cans (14-ounce) Italian-style
   stewed tomatoes (if tomato
   pieces too large cut to preferred
   size)
2 cans Italian-style tomato paste
1 can (14 1/4-ounce) chicken broth
2 tablespoons olive oil
splash of white wine
1 teaspoon Italian seasoning
1/2 teaspoon Schilling basil
1/2 teaspoon Schilling thyme
salt & pepper to taste

Remove Italian sausage from casing and combine with ground turkey. Mix well. In large fry pan brown meat mixture thoroughly.

Drain, then place browned meat in large pot. Add olive oil to fry pan and saute onion and bell pepper. After 1 or 2 minutes add garlic and continue until they are soft.

While onion and bell pepper cook. To meat mixture, add chicken broth, tomatoes, and tomato paste. Stir over medium high heat. When onion mixture is ready, add to meat mixture.

Clean fry pan then add splash of wine and mushrooms saute until done and add to sauce. All ingredients should be in sauce now so just simmer until ready. The longer the better, at least 30 minutes, but 1-2 hours makes a better sauce.

If sauce is too thick, use water or chicken broth to thin. If to thin; add more tomato paste to thicken.

Serve over cooked pasta. I prefer rigatoni or spaghetti.

Vegetarian Main Dishes & Vegetables

No Fail Broccoli Souffle

Paula Zahn

Paula Zahn is co-anchor of CBS This Morning. This recipe was given to her by her mother. "It's no secret that I'm a lousy cook. So when I work up the nerve to make a "real" meal, I go for fool-proof recipes. There is no way you can destroy this dish. It's easy to make. It tastes great fresh out of the oven, and days later as leftovers."

Two packages chopped frozen broccoli
1 1/2 cups Crystal cottage cheese
6 IGA California eggs
1 1/2 cups corn flakes
1/4 grated Kraft cheddar cheese

White Sauce:
1/4 cup Kraft margarine
1 1/2 cups Crystal milk
chopped onion
1/4 cup flour
3/4 cup Kraft sharp cheddar cheese

Cook broccoli in salted water and drain. Put in bottom of three quart baking dish. Make sauce with first 4 ingredients and then add cheddar cheese. Beat together cottage cheese and eggs and combine with sauce. Pour the combination over the broccoli, top with corn flakes and sprinkle with cheddar cheese. Bake at 350° for 40 minutes or until a knife inserted in the center comes out clean. Serves: 12

Low Fat Vegetable Burritos

8 large flour tortillas, burrito-size
2 or 3 medium zucchini, sliced in thin, 3-inch long strips
2 long carrots, cut in thin, 3-inch long strips
1 red and 1 yellow pepper, sliced in thin, 3-inch long strips
1 bunch green onions, sliced thin or 1 medium regular onion, sliced thin and separated into rings
1 cup lettuce, sliced in thin strips
1 can fat-free refried beans
1 1/2 cups cooked rice
1 pint fat-free sour cream
1 avocado
1 teaspoon lemon juice
green chili salsa
green tomatillo sauce, if desired
grated fat-free Kraft cheddar cheese

Susan M. Brown
Sacramento, CA

Peel avocado and mash pulp with a fork. Add 1 teaspoon lemon juice and 2 tablespoons green chili salsa to pulp, stir well and set aside for guacamole.

Stir fry zucchini strips until crisp-tender using a little bit of water in bottom of skillet or wok. Remove zucchini to large plate. Stir fry carrot, pepper, onion and lettuce strips individually until crisp-tender adding water each time a new vegetable is fried. Remove each cooked vegetable to zucchini plate. When all vegetables are fried mix together in skillet or wok to keep warm.

Stir 2 tablespoons green chili salsa into the rice. Slightly warm tortillas between waxed paper in microwave for 20 seconds or warm in pan in oven.

Spread each tortilla with 2 or 3 tablespoons of refried beans, then spoon 2 or 3 tablespoons rice down the center of the tortilla. Layer stir-fried vegetables down the center. Spread vegetables with 2 tablespoons sour cream, 2 tablespoons guacamole and add 1 or 2 tablespoons green chili salsa. Fold bottom up, lap each side over and lay seam-side down on plate. Spread top with tomatillo sauce, if desired, and top with grated cheese.

Artichoke Squares

3 jars marinated artichoke, chopped
3 small bunches green onions
2 cloves garlic
8 IGA California eggs
10 soda crackers, crumbled
1 pound Kraft cheddar cheese
Schilling parsley
dash of tobasco
dash of Worchestershire sauce

Maureen "Mo" Redmond
Folsom, CA

Grate Parmesan cheese and chop green onions. Put oil in pan and lightly fry onions and garlic. Beat eggs in bowl, then add the rest of ingredients. Add just a touch of salt and pepper. Put in a 9x13-inch pan. Bake at 325° for 35 minutes or until firm. Let cool; cut into squares.

Jim's Penne Pomodoro

6 peeled tomatoes
2 cloves garlic, sliced thin
pinch of Schilling oregano and
    Schilling basil
dash of black or white pepper
3 tablespoons Crystal butter
1/4 cup Kraft Parmesan cheese
6 fresh basil leaves chopped
1 pound penne pasta
Kraft Parmesan cheese for garnish

James R Daley
Roseville, CA

Coarsely chop tomatoes. In a saucepan over medium heat, combine chopped tomatoes, garlic, spices and 1 1/2 tablespoons butter or olive oil. Cook for 5-7 minutes uncovered.

Meanwhile, cook the pasta in boiling water, drain, mix with sauce, remaining butter or oil and Parmesan cheese. Garnish with sprinkling of Parmesan and fresh basil (optional). (Olive oil may be substituted for butter.) Serves: 4

Mushroom Souffle

1 pound fresh sliced mushrooms
4 tablespoons Crystal butter or Kraft
    margarine
1/2 cup each chopped green
    pepper, green onions, and celery
1/4 teaspoon salt
1/4 teaspoon Schilling garlic salt
1/4 teaspoon pepper
2 tablespoons Schilling parsley
1/2 cup Kraft mayonnaise
6 slices firm (day old) bread

Eva Holden

82

Remove crust from bread and cut into 1-inch squares. Saute mushrooms for 5 minutes in butter or margarine. Add vegetables, salts and pepper. Cook 3 minutes, remove from heat, stir in mayonnaise. Set aside. Spray or oil a 2 1/2 quarts ovenproof casserole dish. Line sides and bottom with 1/2 bread squares. Spoon mushroom mixture over bread. Cover with remaining bread squares.

Beat together until frothy, 3 eggs, 2 cups milk and 1/2 teaspoon salt. Pour mixture over casserole. Refrigerate covered at least 1 hour (or overnight) Bake uncovered at 325° for 50 minutes. Sprinkle Parmesan cheese over top. Return to oven. Bake 10 minutes. Serves: 6-8

Aegean Green Beans

Ron Paulat

Ron Paulat has been a California resident since 1954, and an art instructor for the last 20 years. As a professional artist he is represented by Michael Himovitz Gallery in Sacramento. His most recent professional activity was as a founding member of "the blage Bros." This recipe is as served in the Attic Restaurant, Athens.

2 pounds green beans
2 tablespoons roasted elephant garlic (finely minced)
2 tablespoons olive oil
big pinch salt
little pinch pepper
4-5 medium tomatoes, peeled and seeded
1 medium onion, finely grated
1/2 cup dry white wine
1 ounce Crystal butter
6 ounces feta cheese
1/2 cup ripe olives
fresh, whole basil leaves

Clean and steam green beans, retaining a certain crispness and good color, plunge into ice water to stop cooking and dry thoroughly. Toss beans with olive oil and garlic, sprinkle with salt and pepper, and arrange laterally on an oblong platter. Chop tomatoes, combine with onion, wine and butter, saute and reduce to a sauce. Allow to cool and pour lengthwise over the center of arranged beans.

Crumble feta cheese over the strip of sauce and garnish platter with olives and basil leaves. Serves: 10-12.

Indonesian Vegetable Pickle

1 cup carrot sticks
1 cup cauliflower sprigs
1 cup green beans
10 red fresh chilies
10 fresh green chilies
1 green cucumber
2 tablespoon peanut oil
2 cloves garlic, finely grated
2 teaspoons finely grated ginger
3 candle nuts or Brazil kernels, grated
1 teaspoon ground turmeric
1/2 cup white vinegar
1/2 cup water
2 teaspoons IGA sugar (at least)
1/2 teaspoon salt (at least)
1/2 teaspoon white pepper

Walter Leidelmeyer
Sacramento, CA

Cut carrots into jullienne strips. Cut beans into pieces of the same length. Then slice each piece in two lengthways. If beans are very young and slender it will not be necessary to slice them. Cut chilies in half lengthwise and remove the seeds. Peel cucumber and cut in half lengthwise, remove seeds and slice in half again lengthwise, cut again into pieces the size as the carrots and beans.

Heat oil in sauce pan and fry grated ginger and grated garlic on low heat for 1 minute. Add grated nuts and turmeric and fry for only a few seconds longer. Add vinegar, water, and salt, sugar, and bring to a boil. Add carrots and beans, chilies and cauliflower sprigs. Return to the boil and boil for 3 minutes. Then add the cucumber and boil for 1 minute longer. Turn into an Earthenware or glass bowl and allow to cool. Use immediately or bottle and store in refrigerator for a week or two. For larger quantities.

Polenta Passion

2 quarts water (salted)
2 cups polenta
2 cups grated Kraft mozzarella
   cheese

Sauce:
2 tablespoons olive oil
1 red onion
3-4 cloves of garlic
1/2 -1 pound sliced mushrooms
2 (16-ounce) cans tomatoes or 6
   large tomatoes finely chopped
1 1/2 teaspoons Schilling oregano
salt and pepper to taste

Robin Song
Auburn, CA

Saute onion, garlic and mushrooms in olive oil in large iron fry pan, (add mushrooms after onions are limp). Add tomatoes, oregano and salt and pepper. Cover and let simmer for 15-20 minutes. In large pan pour in 2 cups polenta to lukewarm salted water. Let this come to a boil and turn to low. Cook and stir for 30 minutes. In large casserole dish layer the polenta, tomato mixture and grated cheese. Bake for 30 minutes. Let set for 15 minutes. Serves: 6-8

Spinach and Rice Pie

1/2 cup rice, cooked to 1 cup
1 medium yellow squash (9-ounce)
spinach, thawed
1 IGA California egg lightly beaten
1/3 cup dry seasoned bread crumbs
2 tablespoons Kraft Parmesan
   cheese

Filling:
3 IGA California eggs lightly beaten
3/4 cup Crystal milk
1/4 cup Kraft Parmesan cheese
1 (10-ounce) package frozen,
   chopped spinach (thawed)
1 cup Kraft sharp cheddar cheese or
   Kraft mozzarella cheese

Kathy Carlson
Fair Oaks, CA

Cook rice. Grate Parmesan cheese, peel and shred squash. Combine rice, squash and spinach in large mixing bowl. Add egg, bread crumbs and cheese. Press into greased 9-inch pie plate or 8x8x2-inch Pyrex pan. In bowl, combine filling ingredients. Put over crust.

Bake 35 minutes at 350° or until center is set. Sprinkle with cheese (Kraft cheddar cheese or Kraft mozzarella cheese or grated Kraft Parmesan cheese) and bake an additional 1 minute. Let stand 10 minutes before cutting. I just let it stand with cheese 11 minutes.

You could add any favorite seasonings to center mixture. You can also substitute chopped broccoli (well drained) but add 1 tablespoon flour when added to center mixture. Using a Pyrex square or rectangle would be good to make hors d'oeuvre size pieces. Prep time: 25 minutes. Cook time: 36 minutes & 10 minutes stand time. Yields: 4-6 servings

Summer Vegetable Delight

California Tomato Growers Association

1/4 pound bacon-cut into 1/2" thick pieces
4 medium squash, any combination of crook neck, green or golden zucchini, cut into 1/2" thick slices
1 yellow onion, cut in half and slice 1/4" thick
2 cups mushrooms, sliced thick
1 pint, or more if desired, chopped stewed tomatoes
2-3 beef bouillon cubes
Seasonings: fresh minced garlic or Schilling garlic powder, sweet basil, salt and pepper to taste

Brown bacon in a 4-quart sauce pot. Before bacon becomes crisp, add minced garlic and squash, lightly brown. Add onions and mushrooms, stir. Add tomatoes and beef bouillon cubes. Stir and add all remaining seasonings. Simmer just until bouillon cubes dissolve and squash is cooked to the desired tenderness. Note: You may vary the vegetables for other family favorites.

Fran's Eggplant

1 medium eggplant
2 large IGA California eggs
1/4 cup water
salt, pepper, cayenne
2 cups bran

Fran Knobloch
Burson, CA

Peel eggplant, slice put in cold water to cover leave 1/2 hour. Beat eggs, water and seasonings to taste. Heat skillet with olive oil. Dip each slice of eggplant in egg mixture then bran. Brown both sides.

Eggs A La Solomon

Russell Solomon

Founder, President and Owner of MTS, Incorporated (d/b/a Tower Records/Video/Books/Galleries). Started MTS in Sacramento in 1960. This recipe originated from a rather empty refrigerator and basic hunger.

olive oil or oil
garlic cloves
handfuls of fresh vegetables chopped into bite size bits (such as mushrooms, onion, tomatoes, zucchini, broccoli, asparagus — almost everything)
spices such as salt, pepper, Schilling oregano, Schilling basil, Schilling parsley
4 IGA California eggs

In large frying pan, saute in oil all vegetables and garlic and cook down until almost soft. Break eggs over top of vegetable mixture making sure not to break the yolks. Cover pan. Just a few minutes until done to your liking That's it!!!

Spinach Florentine

Mary Jane Popp

Radio and TV personality. "First Lady of Radio in Sacto." Columnist "Poppoff" social gossip column. Restaurant reviewer and entertainment "Pennysaver," Snack travel Popp. Recipe passed to me from a dear friend.

2 packages chopped frozen spinach
2 cups Crystal sour cream
2 IGA California eggs
1 cup Kraft Monterey Jack cheese
1 cup Kraft cheddar cheese
1/2 cup Crystal cottage cheese
1/2 cup garlic butter
1 clove chopped garlic
1/2 cup bread crumbs

Mix all ingredients except bread crumbs. Pour creamy mixture into uncovered baking dish. Spread crumbs over top of mixture. Bake at 350° for 45 minutes.

Carrots with Raspberry Vinegar

4-5 carrots, thinly sliced
3 tablespoons water
3 tablespoons Crystal butter
pinch salt
1 tablespoon IGA brown sugar
3 tablespoons raspberry vinegar

Bev Williams
Penn Valley, CA

Put carrots in heavy saucepan with butter and water. Cover and simmer over low heat 15-20 minutes until tender. Add sugar and vinegar, heat through. Garnish with parsley. Serves: 4

Zucchini Casserole

3 pounds fresh zucchini
1 1/2 cup onion
2 cups grated Kraft sharp cheddar
    cheese
1/2 cup Crystal butter
2 teaspoons seasoned salt
1/4 teaspoon tobasco sauce
4 IGA California eggs beaten
3 cups soft bread crumbs
1/4 cup melted Crystal butter

Mary McGuffin
Sierra City, CA

Cut zucchini into 1/2 inch cubes set aside saute onion in the butter until limp. Combine zucchini, onion, cheese, seasoning, and eggs mixing well. Turn into a 2 1/2 quarts buttered casserole. Combine bread crumbs and 1/4 cup melted butter sprinkle over zucchini mixture. Bake uncovered in a 325° oven for 1 hour. Serves: 8

Kitchen Sink Stir-fry

Corydon Ireland

Born in Buffalo, New York, 1947. Master's degree in English. Single parent, two grown daughters. Worked as printer, teacher of composition, freelance writer. Now health and environment reporter with Rochester (N.Y.) Democrat and Chronicle. Nationally syndicated vegetarian columnist, Gannett News Service. His vegetarian recipes appear in The Record of San Joaquin

3 tablespoons olive oil
1/2 onion, chopped
1 green pepper, chopped
3 stalks celery, chopped
1 medium carrot, chopped or grated
1 cup red cabbage, chopped
handful of dry-roasted peanuts
less than a handful of raisins
two nori seaweed sheets (optional)
freshly ground black pepper, to taste
a few drops of sesame oil, to taste
tamari soy sauce, to taste
1 cup brown rice, cooked

Heat oil in wok or deep skillet. Saute vegetables, starting with onions, in order of crispness. Mix each added ingredient freely with hot oil. Add black pepper periodically, in several generous dashes.

A minute or two after last vegetable ingredient is added, add peanuts and raisins in the mix well. Turn off heat. Add crumbled nori sheets into mix and stir in well. Add drops of sesame oil and generous shots of tamari. Add cooked rice (best if slightly dry) last. Mix in well. Serve hot with steamed winter squash and brown bread. Keeps well. Good as a cold dish on the second day. Serves: 4

Zucchini Fretata

Dennis Haworth

This recipe is favorite at our house for breakfast or brunch. It can also be cut into squares and served as an hors d'oeuvre.

5 zucchinis 6-7"
1 large chopped onion, red or white
1 small clove garlic or Schilling garlic
    powder
olive oil
3-4 IGA California eggs
1/4 cup grated Kraft Parmesan
    cheese or Kraft Monterey Jack
    cheese
3 tablespoons water
5-6 large chopped fresh firm mush-
    rooms

Put garlic in enough olive oil to saute onion and sliced zucchini until lightly brown and tender. Add mushrooms. Cook until just tender. Beat Eggs, add water and cheese in separate bowl. Pour egg mixture over zucchini in a skillet over medium heat. Stir a little to get thoroughly mixed. Let sit... When bubbles up, just a few minutes, put under broiler until top browns. Let sit in pan 5 minutes until cools. Flip out onto dish or platter and cut into pie shape pieces or squares. Serves: 4-6

T.J.'s Rice and Veggies

1 carrot sliced in 1/4" round slices
1 stem of broccoli, broken into
   flowerets
1 cup cauliflower, cut into flowerets
1/4 cup water
1 cup pasta sauce
1 1/2 cups cooked brown rice
1/4 cup white wine
1/2 pound ground turkey
1 clove garlic, minced
1/2 cup chopped onion

Joyce Mihanovich
Carmichael, CA

In large saucepan, heat white wine over medium heat. Add crumbled ground turkey, garlic and onions. Saute until onions are shiny and limp and the turkey is no longer pink.

Add carrots, broccoli, cauliflower, water and pasta sauce. Stir well, cover and cook over medium heat for 5-6 minutes. Stir in cooked brown rice, cover and cook for another 8-10 minutes. Add small amounts of water, if necessary, to keep mixture very moist. Serve with dinner rolls and green salad. Serves: 4

Stuffed Eggplant on the Half Shell

1 medium eggplant split lengthwise
salt and pepper to taste
3 ounces Crystal butter or Kraft
   margarine
1 cup Crystal milk
1 cup celery, chopped
1 tablespoon onion, chopped
1/2 cup grated Kraft cheddar
   cheese
1 cup Ritz type crackers, crumbled

Betty Crandall

Scoop inside from eggplant and cook in salted water until tender. Drain well and season with salt and pepper. Add the remaining ingredients to mixture and return mixture to shells. Place shells in baking pan. Add additional grated cheese and cracker crumbs to top of each shell. Bake uncovered 1 hour at 350°. Serves: 4-6

German Spinach

1 package chopped spinach,
   cooked
3 slices bacon
3/4 cup Crystal milk
1 1/2 tablespoons flour
1/2 teaspoon salt
1/4 teaspoon Schilling nutmeg
1 tablespoon chopped onion,
   optional

Doris Strange
Atwater, CA

Fry bacon; set aside to cool. Put flour into the hot fat and stir vigorously. Pour in milk to make a thick gravy. Add salt, nutmeg and chopped onions. Pour gravy over hot, cooked drained spinach. Toss gently. Top with crumbled bacon.

Tortilla Squash Casserole

1 1/4 cups shredded Kraft cheddar
   cheese
3/4 cup Crystal cottage cheese
4-6 thin slices nonfat Kraft Swiss
   cheese
4 corn tortillas
2-3 summer squash (sliced and
   steamed until tender)

Louise Zimmerman
Sacramento, CA

Layer tortillas with shredded cheddar cheese, cottage cheese, squash slices, and Swiss cheese. Top with some of the Swiss cheese and a little of the shredded cheddar. Place casserole in 375° oven for about 20-25 minutes or until cheese begins to bubble. Cut in sections with sharp knife and serve. Serves: 3-4

Vegetables Primavera

4 cups vegetables and combination
   or the following:
Chopped broccoli, cauliflower,
   celery, cabbage, onions, or green
   peppers
Sliced mushrooms or carrots, pea
   pods, green beans
1 jar (28-ounce) spaghetti sauce
   (less than 4 grams of fat per 4-
   ounce)
2 1/2 cups cooked spaghetti
   noodles

Deon Seawell

Microwave Method: mix all ingredients, cover and cook on high for 15 minutes. Stirring at 5 minute intervals. Cook longer if you prefer vegetables to be less crisp. Serve over spaghetti noodles. Serves: 5

Stove top Method: Mix all ingredients, cover and simmer until vegetables are cooked to preferred tenderness. Serve over spaghetti noodles.

Jarlesbery Cheese Vegetable Bake

1 medium eggplant, sliced
1/4 cup Wesson oil
3 medium zucchini, sliced
1 cup sliced fresh mushrooms
1/2 cup green pepper strips (Bell)
1/2 cup green onions (sliced)
1 medium clove garlic, minced
1 cup halved cherry tomatoes
2 cups shredded Jarlesbery cheese
   or Kraft Swiss cheese

Barbara Ann Forman
Sacramento, CA

Saute zucchini, mushrooms, green onion, green peppers, also garlic in some oil for several minutes, just until softening. Add tomatoes, salt, pepper alternate layers of vegetables and cheese in a buttered shallow 2 quarts baking dish, ending with cheese. Bake in 350° oven for 30 minutes until cheese is melted and vegetables are tender. Serves: 4-6

Meatless Meatballs

1 cup grated Kraft sharp cheddar
   cheese
3/4 cup ground walnuts
2 cups fine crackers crumbs
2 tablespoons Schilling minced
   onion
1 clove mined garlic
1 tablespoon dry Schilling parsley
1 teaspoon Worchestershire sauce
6 IGA California eggs

Yvonne Sinclair
Rocklin, CA

Mix ingredients together well. Make into balls and saute. Place in a casserole with tomato sauce or mushroom soup. Sour cream added to the mushroom soup give a "Stroganoff" flavor. Make into a loaf and cover with tomato sauce. Cook 375° for 30 minutes or until hot through.

Servings: can be made into small "meatloaf" or meat ball servings for 4.

Gnocchi di Spinaci

Luigi Bomparola-Il Fornaio

Luigi Bomparola is a third generation chef from a Milanese family, cooking since he was 12. At 24 years old he opened Il Fornaio in Beverly Hills as the Executive Chef.

Gnocchi:
1 bunch of spinach
2 large Idaho potatoes
1 cup of flour
2 IGA California eggs
2 tablespoons grated Kraft Parmesan
   cheese
1/4 teaspoon Schilling nutmeg
a pinch of salt and pepper

Tomato Sauce:
2 tablespoons olive oil
1 teaspoon chopped garlic
1 pound roma tomatoes
1 cup of marinara sauce
6 basil leaves, washed and chopped

Steam spinach for 3 minutes and then drain. Place potatoes in boiling water until cooked, then peel.

Puree spinach and potatoes together until smooth. Then pour mixture onto a clean flat surface and form a circle with a hollow center.

Then add four, eggs, Parmesan, nutmeg, salt and pepper. Knead dough until it becomes well mixed and smooth. Sprinkle four on top of the ball of dough. Then allow dough to sit for a few minutes.

Roll dough into 1/2" round logs and then cut into 1" long gnocchi. To cook gnocchi, add to furiously boiling water for a few minutes until they rise to the surface.

To store gnocchi: four a cookie sheet and set gnocchi on cookie sheet. Once gnocchi have been frozen for at least an hour, the gnocchi may be stored in a plastic bag and stored in freezer.

For sauce: place oil in pan, then add garlic until browned. Add chopped Roma tomatoes and marinara sauce.

Cook for 2 minutes. Then add gnocchi (already cooked). Add chopped basil immediately before serving.

Place in dish and add a basil leaf for decoration.
Serves: 4

90

German Red Cabbage

1 head of red cabbage
1/2 cup IGA white sugar
1/2 cup IGA brown sugar
4 tablespoons Crystal butter
1 Granny Smith apple
1 cup white vinegar
10-20 whole cloves

Judith Ann Clemons
Lodi, CA

dice or shred red cabbage and Granny Smith apple. Add all ingredients in large soup pot and simmer together 4 to 5 hours. Excellent served with holiday turkey, chicken or pork. Serves: 12

Eggplant-Zucchini A La Greco

Mayor Joan Darrah

For eggplant and lamb aficionados, this is an excellent casserole. Serve with green salad and french bread.

2 medium-size (about 2 1/2 pound total) eggplants, ends trimmed
4 medium-size (about 1 pound total) zucchini, ends trimmed
about 1 tablespoon olive or oil
1 package (1 pound, 3 ounces) firm tofu
1 package (1 pound) nonfat cottage cheese
8 ounces (about 2 cups) mozzarella cheese, shredded
1 cup cooked white or brown rice
1/2 teaspoon fennel seed, crushed
1/2 -1 teaspoon crushed dried hot red chilis, optional
About 3 tablespoons grated Parmesan cheese

Lamb sauce:
4 cloves garlic, minced
1 medium size brown onion chopped
1 tablespoon olive oil
1 pound ground lamb
1/4 teaspoon garlic salt
1 (28-ounce) can peeled pear shaped tomatoes with basil
1 (15-ounce) can tomato sauce
1/2 teaspoon oregano
1/2 teaspoon bail
1/2 teaspoon salt

Cut eggplants crosswise into 1/2 inch slices; cut zucchini lengthwise into 1/4 inch slices. Lay in single layer in 3 oiled pans, each 10 by 15 inches (or bake in sequence). Bake in a 400° oven until soft and golden brown, 30 minutes (turn after 15).

Meanwhile, slice tofu; lay between paper towels. Press to release excess liquid. Mash tofu in a bowl; add cottage cheese, mozzarella, rice, and fennel.

Spoon 1 cup lamb sauce (recipe following) into oiled 9x13-inch baking dish. Layer 1/2 of the eggplants, zucchinis, and tofu mixture, and 2 cups lamb sauce; repeat layers. Sprinkle with Parmesan. Bake in a 400° oven until hot, about 45 minutes. Let rest 15 minutes before serving.

Lamb Sauce: Saute garlic in olive oil and add chopped onion and saute five minutes. Add lamb and garlic salt and cook until brown. Add all other ingredients and simmer 20 minutes. Serves: 10

Meats, Poultry & Fish

Bender's "Out and About" Chuck Roast

Dave Bender

News 10 weatherman Dave Bender joined KXTV from KTIG-TV (Fox) in Washington, D.C. He also worked at KNBC-TV in Los Angeles and KNSD-TV in San Diego. Bender is best known for his humor and ability to deliver the weather in a fun and friendly manner.

roast
onion soup mix
2 cans golden mushroom soup
vegetables: Idaho potatoes, celery, carrots, mushrooms, corn

For crock pot: Before you go "out and about" for the day, put roast in pot (cut off small bones), top with 1 package onion soup mix. Add 2 cans golden mushroom soup. Add veggies. Cook all day on low.

Sloppy Joes

6 sliced hamburger buns
1 pound ground beef
1 can (10.5 ounces) tomato soup
1 tablespoon prepared mustard
1/2 teaspoons salt, optional

Leslie Ruff
Merced, CA

Brown ground beef in skillet. Drain grease. Stir in soup, mustard and salt. Simmer over low heat for 10 minutes, stirring occasionally. Spoon into buns.

Chicken Enchilada

12 corn tortilla shells
3-4 whole chicken breasts-cooked and shredded
large package of Kraft cream cheese
2 tablespoons Wesson oil
1 tablespoon red wine vinegar
2-8 ounce cans tomato sauce
chopped onions to taste
1 can chopped chilis
salt, pepper, garlic
crushed red pepper, white cheese

Pam Nelson
Auburn, CA

Fry tortilla shells for just a few seconds, then drain. In large baking dish, put chicken in shells with some cream cheese. Simmer oil, vinegar, tomato sauce, onions, chilis, salt, pepper, garlic and red pepper for approximately 15 minutes on low heat. Pour sauce mixture over shells stuffed with chicken and cream cheese. Top all with shredded white cheese. Bake in a preheated 350° oven for 30 minutes. Makes: 12 Enchiladas

Scrumptious Shrimp Scampi

Cynder Sinclair

Cynder Sinclair is the Executive Director San Joaquin County Child Abuse Prevention Council. This recipe has been a favorite in Cynder's family for over 3 generations because not only is it quick to prepare for a family meal, but it is perfect for a dinner party.

1 pound large shelled shrimp
2 sticks Crystal butter
6 large cloves garlic, minced
dash tabasco
dash Worchestershire
1 tablespoon chopped fresh parsley
1 tablespoon chopped fresh dill
    weed
Kraft Parmesan cheese

Melt butter in a heavy skillet, saute garlic, add shrimp, tabasco and Worchestershire. Cook until shrimp is pin. Remove from heat. Stir in parsley and dill weed. Put into ovenproof baking dish, sprinkle top with Parmesan cheese. Bake at 400° for 10 minutes. Bask in the rave reviews. Serves: 4

Garlic Baste for Roast Turkey

6 cloves garlic
1 tablespoon Schilling paprika
1/2 teaspoon salt
1/4 teaspoon pepper
1/4 cup Wesson oil

Helen Murphy
Stockton, CA

Mince garlic cloves in garlic press. Add rest of ingredients. Brush basting sauce all over turkey and inside body cavity. Place turkey breast down on rack in roasting pan. Roast at 325° according to directions or size of turkey. When turkey is about half done, turn bird on it's back. Baste until done. Tis also works well for whole turkey breast.

Uncle Lewy's Pork Chops & Gravy

4-6 thick pork chops
1/2 pound mushrooms, sliced
1 large onion, quartered and sliced
2 slices bacon, chopped
1 (10-ounce) can cream of mush-
    room soup
1 (10-ounce) can milk
2 tablespoons Worcestershire sauce
flour
salt and pepper
2 cloves garlic, crushed

Neal Lewis
Newcastle, CA

Fry bacon until almost crisp, remove. Dust chops in flour, salt and pepper. Brown chops in bacon grease and remove. Saute onions, garlic and mushrooms until almost done, remove. Return chops to pan. Top with onions, mushrooms, garlic and bacon. Mix soup and milk and worchestershire sauce and pour on top. Cover and simmer slow for 20 minutes. Remove, cover. Mix lightly and simmer for 10 more minutes to reduce gravy serve with mashed potatoes, and lock the doors! Serves: 4-6

Barbecue Chicken

4-6 skinless chicken breasts
Italian salad dressing
dijon mustard
seasoned salt
pepper (according to your own taste preferences)

First baste chicken on both sides with mustard, then baste with salad dressing, seasoned salt and pepper. Place chicken on grill and sear until meat turns from pink to white on both sides. Baste once again with some ingredients and continue grilling until meat is done. Enjoy!!!

Governor Pete Wilson

"My wife, Gayle, and I are delighted to share a recipe for one of our favorite dishes. I think you will find it a simple and delicious way to prepare chicken."

Basil-Crusted Chicken Oriental

6 premium boneless, skinless split chicken breasts
4 tablespoons Crystal butter or Kraft margarine, melted
2 tablespoons Hoisin sauce*
1 tablespoon plus 1 teaspoon Chinese style hot mustard
2/3 cup Panko Japanese style bread crumbs*, or plain dry bread crumbs
3 tablespoons chopped fresh basil or 1 tablespoon dried Schilling basil (fresh basil preferred)
2 tablespoons grated Kraft Parmesan cheese
2 small plum tomatoes, peeled, diced and divided
fresh basil and plum tomatoes, garnish

Tomato Mustard Cream Sauce:
1/2 cup light or regular dairy Crystal sour cream
2 tablespoons tomato paste
2 teaspoons Chinese style hot mustard
1 teaspoon light soy sauce

Preheat oven to 500°. Rinse chicken breasts and pat dry. Combine butter, Hoisin sauce and mustard in a wide, shallow dish. Mix bread crumbs, basil and cheese in another shallow dish. Dip each chicken breast in butter mixture, then in bread crumb mixture, coating well on all sides. Place in a single layer in a shallow, nonstick baking pan. Bake uncovered at 500°. for 15 minutes, or until crumb coating is golden brown and chicken tests done.

Prepare Tomato Mustard Cream Sauce by combining sour cream, tomato paste, mustard and soy sauce. Blend well then stir in half the diced tomatoes. Heat in microwave oven on HIGH power for 30 seconds, or heat in a saucepan just until warmed.

Spoon sauce onto warmed serving platter. Place whole chicken breasts over sauce, or cut breasts crosswise into thick slices and arrange over sauce. Sprinkle chicken with remaining diced tomato. Garnish with basil and plum tomatoes if desired. *Available in oriental food section of supermarket. Serves: 6

Teresa Hannan Smith
Sacramento, CA

Slocum House Corn and Lobster Waffle

1 21-ounce can corn, drained
7 tablespoons flour
1/2 ounce bacon, diced and
    cooked
1 teaspoon baking powder
3 each IGA California eggs
1 pinch salt
1 pinch white pepper
18 ounces lobsters, cooked
4 tablespoons tomatoes, diced
1 teaspoon garlic, chopped
2 tablespoons basil, fresh
1/2 cup Crystal cream
1 dash lemon juice
1 dash salt and pepper

Place corn, bacon, eggs, flour, baking powder, salt and pepper in a blender and blend until just mixed (do not over blend), then let sit for one hour. Pour small amount of batter into hot waffle iron. Let cook until steam stops rising.

In a small sauce pan reduce cream, garlic and lemon juice until thick. Add basil, tomatoes and lobster. Toss until lobster is just hot (don't over cook). Adjust seasoning and pour over hot waffle then serve immediately. Serves: 6

Cashew Chicken

1 (5-ounce) can chow mein noodles
2 cups diced cooked chicken
3/4 cup chopped celery
1/2 cup chopped green onion
1 can cream of mushroom soup
1 cup cashews
3/4 cup chicken broth

Boil chicken and save broth. Set aside 1/2 cup crisp noodles. Combine remaining ingredients and place in greased 2 quart casserole. Sprinkle reserved noodles over top. Bake 325° for 30 minutes.

Janet L. Berreth
Lodi, CA

Red Snapper and Tomatoes

California Tomato Growers Association

2 onions, sliced and browned in Wesson oil
1 pound (12-ounce) can of toma-
    toes, drained
1 small jar pimientos, diced
2 tablespoons capers
1-3 ounce jar green olives
salt and pepper
2 pounds red snapper cut into
    serving pieces

Combine onion and tomatoes and simmer for 10 minutes. Place fish in a buttered casserole dish with pimientos, capers, green olives, salt and pepper. Pour onions and tomatoes over fish. Bake at 350° for 25-30 minutes.

Slick Dumplings

Y.A. Tittle

Y.A. Tittle began his professional football career after being Baltimore's first draft pick in the All-American Conference in 1948. Joined the 49'ers in 1951. Traded to New York in 1961 and led the Giants to three straight Eastern Division titles. Inducted in the professional Hall of Fame in 1971.

1 whole chicken
2 cups flour
Crystal butter or Kraft margarine
2 cups flour
salt and pepper, to taste)
1 cube of Crystal butter or Kraft
  margarine

Place whole chicken in large pot. Cover with water and bring to boil. Boil until chicken is tender. Remove chicken from broth. When chicken is cool enough, remove from bones and cut into bite-sized pieces.

In mixing bowl combine flour, salt, pepper and butter. Mix it together with your hands until it is the consistency of fine crumbs.

Pour some of the hot chicken broth (1 to 2 cups) into the flour mixture until it is glazed enough to form a ball. Flour cutting board and add flour over ball until it is firm enough to roll out. Cut into squares.

Take remaining hot chicken broth, add 1 cube of butter (or margarine) and bring to boil. Drop squares of dough into boiling chicken broth and cook for 10 minutes. Add chicken broth and cook 5 minutes. Adjust salt and pepper to taste. Serve immediately.
Serves: 4

Lobster Sauce For Baked Or Sauteed Salmon

Alan Wilcox-Headquarter House Restaurant

Alan Wilcox was born in Princeton, New Jersey. He graduated from Hobbart College in Geneva, New York. Alan relocated to San Francisco where he worked as a special events chef for the Tiger Club and later moved to the foothills where he work under French trained chef, Micheal Hammonds. Alan was head chef at Hummers Fine Food.

Shells only of 3-4 lobsters, or substitute 1-2 tablespoons of lobster
  paste (available at specialty
  stores)
1 carrot, rough cut
1 celery stalk, rough cut
1/2 onion, rough cut
1 clove garlic, chopped
2-3 tablespoons olive oil
1 ounce brandy
1 cup white wine
2 cups Crystal cream
2-3 tablespoons Crystal butter

In heavy, 2-quart sauce pan place olive oil, lobster shells vegetables and garlic, saute' over medium high heat for 1-2 minutes moving constantly so ingredients do not char.

Add brandy and flame, use caution. When flames subside, add white wine. Reduce heat and simmer slowly until wine is 3/4 reduced. Add cream, simmer gently for 15-20 minutes or longer until all flavors come through.

Strain through fine sieve and add whole butter to melt prior to serving. Salt and pepper to taste. For deeper reddish color, add 2 tablespoons tomato paste with the wine.

Joyce's Garlic Chicken

Joyce Raley Teel

Joyce Raley Teel was involved in the Crocker Art Museum, the American Heart Association, the Children's Home Guild, the Cerebral Palsy Guild and the Senior Gleaners as a homemaker. In 1986, along with Raley's President/CEO Charles L. Collings, she organized Food For Families, a nonprofit food distribution program feeding the hungry throughout Raley's area of service. Joyce Raley Teel serves as president of Food For Families.

3 1/2 pounds chicken, skin removed (I prefer thighs)
3 tablespoons peanut oil (to make fat-free, use a cooking spray)
1 bulb (not clove) fresh garlic, peeled and coarsely chopped
2 small dried hot red peppers (optional)
3/4 cup distilled white vinegar
1/4 cup soy sauce
3 tablespoons honey

In heavy skillet, brown chicken on all sides, add garlic. Add peppers near the end of browning if desired.

Add remaining ingredients and cook over medium-high heat until chicken is done and sauce has been reduced somewhat. This will not take long, less than 10 minutes.

If you are using both white and dark meat, remove white meat first, so it does not dry out. Watch very carefully so that sauce does not burn or boil away.

There should be a quantity of sauce left to serve with the chicken. Chicken should appear slightly glazed.

Serve with Chinese noodles, pasta or rice. Serves: 4 to 6

Chicken and Grapes

4 chicken breasts
1 fresh lemon
Wesson oil for frying
1 cup chicken gravy
1/2 cup dry white wine
1 cup button mushrooms
1 teaspoon Schilling curry powder
1/4 teaspoon Schilling ginger
1/4 teaspoon Schilling allspice
1 cup white seedless grapes
1/4 cup almond slivers (optional)

J. Allen Miller, M.D.
Sacramento, CA

Rub chicken pieces with fresh lemon generously at least 1 hour ahead of time. Brown chicken in oil. Either make gravy from pan drippings or use canned chicken gravy and add the wine, mushrooms, and browned chicken along with the spices. Cook until chicken is done and tender (about 20-40 minutes).

About 5-10 minutes before serving, add the grapes and almond slivers. Serves: 4

Baked Salmon with Asian Herbs

Jan Mendelson

Chinois East/West

Chef Jan Mendelson, like many of the founders of California cuisine, began cooking professionally while in school, and left academia for a culinary career. After stints at a number of restaurants, Chef Mendelson came to Chinois East/West in 1988. In this adaptation of Saumon au Vert, a traditional Thai seasoning paste of cilantro, garlic, and pepper is used, enlivened by the addition of mint and basil, and complemented by a ginger and rice wine beurre blanc.

1/4 cup minced garlic
1/4 cup finely chopped cilantro
   (leaves and stems)
1/4 cup finely chopped fresh basil
   (leaves)
1/4 cup finely chopped fresh mint
   (leaves)
1/4 cup safflower (or other light) oil
1 tablespoon freshly cracked black
   pepper
1/4 teaspoons salt
4 - 8 ounces salmon fillets
1 tablespoon Wesson oil
2 tablespoons white wine
1/4 cup sake
1/4 cup white wine vinegar
6 tablespoons unseasoned rice
   vinegar
1/4 cup fish stock or clam juice
1 tablespoon IGA sugar
1 tablespoon minced shallots
3 tablespoons minced ginger
1 teaspoon minced garlic
1/2 pound Crystal butter, cut in 1"
   pieces
fresh lemon juice
cilantro sprigs and pink pickled
   ginger (sushi ginger) for garnish

Combine garlic, cilantro, basil, mint, 1/4 cup oil, black pepper, and salt. Preheat the oven to 375°.

Divide evenly between the 4 salmon fillets, pressing the herb mixture onto the top of each fillet. Heat 1 tablespoon oil in an ovenproof saute pan large enough to hold the 4 fillets. Place the salmon in the pan, herb side up, and sear the bottom 1 minute.

Place the pan in the oven and bake about 7 minutes for medium rare, or until cooked to desired doneness.

In the meantime, prepare the sauce. Combine the white wine, sake, white wine vinegar, rice vinegar, fish stock, sugar, shallots, ginger, and garlic in a small sauce pan and reduce until syrupy.

Remove from heat, and quickly whisk in butter, a few pieces at a time. When all the butter has been emulsified, the sauce should be about the consistency of heavy cream. Taste, and add a little lemon juice as needed.

Divide the sauce between 4 plates, and place 1 fillet on each. Garnish with cilantro sprigs and pink pickled ginger. New potatoes lightly seasoned with lemon and butter, and steamed broccoli, make excellent accompaniments. Serves: 4

Chicken Wrapped in Bacon

Lloyd Moseby

Married, three kids, wife Adrienne, Alicia (11), Lloyd II (9), Lydell (3). Signed out of High School 1978 with Toronto Blue Jay's. Came up to Majors in 1980. Played with Jay's for 10 years. In 1990 I signed with Detroit Tigers, Played there for 2 years. Then in 1992-93 I played in Tokyo Japan.

chicken breast, boneless (4-5)
1 can cream of mushroom soup
1 small or medium Crystal sour
   cream
6 pieces bacon
salt to taste

Boil breast to remove any fat the chicken might have meanwhile mix cream of mushroom and sour cream together. When ready 20 to 25 minutes. Remove and rinse chicken (Pat dry with towel). Wrap chicken with bacon, secure it with toothpick. Repeat for others, always cook two extra pieces of bacon. Pour the mushroom sour cream sauce over chicken then crumble extra bacon on top. Bake 375° - 400°, 20-25 minutes salt to taste. Serves: 4

Chicken Cordon Bleu

6 boneless chicken breast
3 slices lowfat Kraft Swiss chees
Turkey ham (3 slices each cut in half)
1 cup flour seasoned to taste with
   Schilling garlic powder and fresh
   ground pepper.
2 cans chicken stock (use reduced
   salt if using canned stock)

Linda Borden
Sacramento, CA

Pound breast until about 1/4 inch thick. Coat lightly with seasoned flour. Place one slice of ham and cheese on top and roll up securing with toothpicks. Brown lightly in a hot pan with a small amount of olive oil. After breasts are browned add chicken stock and cook on medium heat for 30-35 minutes. Arrange on platter and garnish with white sauce seasoned with Italian seasoning to taste. Enjoy! Serves: 4-6

Italian Chicken Marinade

Marinade:
2 cups Sauterne wine
1 cup water
1/4 cup Balsamic vinegar
1/4 cup brandy
2 tablespoons Italian seasoning
4 teaspoons poultry seasoning
2 teaspoons onion salt
1 teaspoon garlic pepper
1 teaspoon Schilling oregano
2 teaspoons black pepper
4 cloves of garlic, minced

Dennis F. Spain

Mix and incorporate marinade ingredients in large bowl, add meat, and refrigerate.

Serving Suggestion: After 2 hours remove from refrigeration, meat and marinade. Place chicken with marinade in baking dish. Bake in preheated oven at 350° for approximately 45-55 minutes or until done.

Cajun Trout

Allen E. Johnson

Allen Johnson, City Manager, City of Roseville. Mr. Johnson has been the city manager for six out of the eleven years he has worked for the city. (Recipe taken from "What's Cookin' in Old Station" cook book)

1/4 cup Crystal butter, melted
1/4 cup Wesson oil
1 1/2 teaspoons Schilling paprika
1 teaspoon salt
1/2 teaspoon onion powder
3 cloves garlic, minced or pressed
large bunch parsley
4 to 6 (10 to 12") trout
1/2 teaspoon Schilling cayenne
    pepper
1/4 teaspoon white pepper
1/4 teaspoon black pepper
1/4 teaspoon dried Schilling thyme
1/4 teaspoon dried Schilling oregano

Mix together all ingredients except trout and parsley. Depending on number and size of trout, make pan of heavy-duty foil, 2 layers thick with 1 inch sides. Brush trout inside and out with Cajun mixture. Stuff trout with some of the parsley and put rest of parsley in bottom of foil pan. Lay trout on parsley in foil pan. Place foil pan on grill over hot coals. Cook until fish flakes, being careful not to get too hot a fire as fish may burn on bottom. Serves: 4-6

California Stir Fry

new potatoes, unpeeled, sliced
    thinly
broccoli
carrots
green onions
pea pods
water chestnuts
chicken breasts, pre-boiled, cut in
    small chunks
2 tablespoons teriyaki sauce — add
    more for larger quantities
2 tablespoons water

Kacey Herbst
Sacramento, CA

A quick low-calorie scrumptious dish for the busy working gal or guy This is also good for a "group activity — like cutting up all the veggies. Amounts vary as to number of people.

Spray skillet or wok with Pam or similar product after pan is hot. Put in heavier vegetables first, cook 2 minutes or so, add other vegetables, cook until barely tender, add chicken and liquids. Cover, steam about 2 minutes.

103

Garry's Barbecue Sauce

Garry St. Jean

On May 22, 1992. St. Jean accomplished a life-long ambition as he was named the 17th head coach in the Sacramento Kings' 45-year franchise history. St. Jean and his wife, Mary Jane, and two children. Emily (6) and Gregory (3) reside in Granite Bay. California.

1 cup Wesson oil
1 cup ketchup
1/2 cup white vinegar
4 teaspoons salt
2 tablespoons IGA sugar
4 tablespoons Schilling mustard

Pour all ingredients into a blender and mix until smooth and blended together. Use as barbecue sauce for chicken, pork, or ribs.

Glazed Double Loin of Pork

2 (4-pound) loins of pork
1 box curried rice mix
1/2 cup onion, chopped
2 tablespoons melted Crystal butter
3 tablespoons parsley, minced
1 can tomato sauce
1/4 cup orange liqueur (optional)
1/2 cup catsup
1/2 cup vinegar
1/3 cup IGA brown sugar
1/2 cup light corn syrup
1 cup condensed consomme
1 tablespoon corn starch

Katherine Spencer
Kelseyville , CA

Bone pork loins. Cook rice as directed. Saute onions in butter until brown.

Add onions and parsley to rice. Cool.

Place pork loin fat side down on cutting board after you have lengths of string long enough to tie the two loins together. Season.

Spoon rice on top pressing together well, keeping rice as level as possible.

Place other loin, fat side up, on top of the rice. Tie together tightly with twine; every 2". Place on roasting rack. Bake at 350° for 35 minutes to the pound.

Mix catsup, vinegar, brown sugar, corn syrup, and consomme.

Bring to boil and simmer 5 minutes. Mix corn starch with cold water and cook several minutes until slightly thickened. Add liqueur and simmer 15 minutes.

Before pork is done (40 minutes before), pour off drippings. Place pork in pan. Pour 1/3 of glaze over meat and roast 20 minutes.

Repeat. Baste occasionally. Heat remaining glaze. Serve.

Turkey Chalupus

12 flour tortillas
3 cups turkey breast cooked and cubed
1 can cream of chicken soup
1 can cream of celery soup
1 7-ounce diced green chilis
1 pint Crystal sour cream
3/4 pound Kraft Monterey Jack cheese, grated
3/4 pound Kraft cheddar cheese grated
1 can sliced olives
1 small onion grated
2 teaspoons ground Schilling cumin
green onion tops diced - some, no specific amount

Put together soups, chilis, sour cream, cumin, green onion tops, olives, onion and 1/2 of cheeses, (mixed together) set aside 1 1/2 cups of this mixture on each tortilla and roll up.

Put in greased 9x5-inch baking dish. Put rest of sauce over top. (That's the 1 1/2 cups you didn't add turkoy to)

Sprinkle with remaining cheeses and green onion.

Sprinkle paprika on top.

Refrigerate overnight.

Bake 350° for 45 minutes, uncovered. Goes great with fruit salad.

Sandra Smoley

Sandra Smoley is the Secretary of the California Health and Welfare Agency

Chicken Picatta

chicken breasts (or whole cut up pieces)
1/2 cube Crystal butter
flour
12 green onions, chopped
fresh mushrooms
1/2 cup lemon juice
1/2 cup Sauterne
salt
pepper
Schilling garlic powder
Kraft Parmesan cheese

Jeanne M. Wilkins
Stockton, CA

Flour pieces of chicken and place in 8x12-inch baking pan. Melt butter and pour over chicken. Bake in oven at 350° until chicken is brown. Mix lemon juice, seasonings, and wine and pour over chicken. Add mushrooms and green onions. Cover and bake at 350° for 30 minutes. Sprinkle with cheese and serve. (Parmesan cheese can be added 10-15 minutes before removing chicken from oven.) Serves: 4-6

Orange Roughy with Orange Sauce

AB Cramlet — AB's Cafe

I was born and raised in Ethiopia. I came to the United States in 1977. A mother of six, I love to cook in fresh herbs and create new things. I became a United States citizen by choice in 1986 and I am very proud of it.

1 pound orange roughy fillets, about
    1/2 inch thick
1/2 cup lowfat Crystal milk
1/4 teaspoon salt
1/3 cup all-purpose flour
2 tablespoons and 1 teaspoon olive
    oil or Wesson oil
1 tablespoon finely chopped garlic
4 tablespoons fresh lime juice
2 tablespoons fresh lemon juice
3 tablespoons fresh orange juice
1 tablespoon finely chopped parsley
2 teaspoons snipped chives, or finely
    chopped green onion tops
1 tablespoon unsalted butter

Let fillets soak in milk in shallow dish for 10 minutes. Remove fish from milk; sprinkle with salt. Dredge fish in flour, shaking off excess, oil.

Heat the 2 tablespoons oil in a large skillet over moderately high heat. Add fish; cook until golden brown on one side, about 3 minutes. Carefully turn fish over; cook second side until golden brown and fish is cooked through, 3-4 minutes longer.

Remove fish to serving platter. Wipe skillet clean. Reduce temperature to low. Add remaining teaspoon oil to skillet. Add garlic, cook 30 seconds. Add lime, lemon and orange juices, parsley and chives. Add butter; swirl skillet until just creamy. Pour sauce over fish and serve immediately, with Light Rice or Riso Pasta and vegetable. Serves: 4

Herb Roasted Pheasant with VinBlanc Sauce

Chris and Patty Bogle

Chris Bogle is a third generation Delta farmer who, through the years, has established a ranch of over 800 acres of grapes. His wife, Patty, is general manager of Bogle Winery, which Chris and his father, Warren, founded in 1979. The winery produces over 60,000 cases of fine varietal wines each year, which are distributed in 38 states and four countries abroad. Privately, the Bogle family continues a long tradition of fishing and hunting, and enjoys cooking and preparing the wild game and fish for friends and family.

2 whole pheasants
4-6 slices bacon
2 shallots
3 cloves garlic
1/4 cup + 2 tablespoons fresh basil
2 tablespoons fresh rosemary
2 tablespoons fresh sage
6 slices bacon
4 cups dry white wine
8 ounces Crystal butter
1 small fresh tomato

Finely mince garlic and shallots. Add chopped basil, rosemary and sage (use fresh only). Stuff this mixture between the skin and breast of the pheasants.

Cover each with bacon. Bake in 375 oven for 20-25 minutes or until meat is still slightly pink. (Take bacon off last five minutes to brown skin)

Slice pheasants in half and cover with Vin Blanc sauce. We serve with couscous and grilled vegetables.

VinBlanc sauce: Put white wine in a saucepan, bring to a boil and cook over medium heat until reduced to one half cup. Take off heat and strain into top of double boiler with hot water in bottom. Add butter one ounce at a time, whisking after each addition. Add one small fresh chopped tomato, 2 tablespoons basil chopped, salt and white pepper to taste.

Note: Fresh pheasant is preferable, you will find it at most Asian and specialty markets. Our local community has a children's support group, Friends of the Clarksburg Youth (FOCY), which sponsors a pheasant hunt club to raise funds each year. Serves: 4

Salmon Bitok

Robert Perez

Holbrooke Hotel • Restaurant • Saloon

Salmon:
1 pound salmon meat, diced
1 ounce diced red onion
1 teaspoon fresh chopped thyme
1 pinch chopped garlic
1 tablespoon parsley, chopped
3 basil leaves, cut
1 teaspoon olive oil
salt & pepper to taste
1/2 lemon

Bread Crust Topping:
* 1/2 cup bread crumbs
* parsley, basil, dill, garlic, sun dried

tomatoes, orange zest, nicoise olives (pitted), all to flavor
Place all ingredients in food processor, blend until fine

Piperade:
olive oil
1 cup each red & green bell peppers, cut in thin strips
1/2 bulb anise, cut in thin strips
1 small onion, cut in thin strips
2 tomatoes, chopped
2 cloves garlic, chopped
2 cups orange juice
2 bay leaves
1 pinch crushed red dried chilis
1 pinch cracked black peppercorns

Serves: 4

Turkey Alla Vino (Italian)

1 turkey breast to make 12 slices
15 fresh mushrooms, quartered
4 ounces prosciutto, diced
1/4 pound Crystal butter, melted
4 tablespoons lemon juice
1 cup chicken broth
1/4 cup white wine
pinch of Schilling basil, fresh parsley
    and garlic, chopped

Rose A. Cummings
Woodland, CA

Pound turkey very thin. Coat with unseasoned flour. Brown garlic and prosciutto in butter. Add turkey pieces brown on both sides. Add seasoning, wine, lemon juice and chicken broth. Simmer for 3 to 5 minutes. Serve with spaghetti or rice. Serves: 4

Ginger Marinated Swordfish Brochette

Sherri Smith

Wine and Roses Country Inn Hotel and Restaurant

Sherri Smith, of the Wine and Roses Country Inn Hotel and Restaurant, grew up in Palo Alto, attended UCSB, graduated from California Culinary Academy in San Francisco. A business full of appreciative guests has shaped her sense of food style with simple, yet elegant, entertaining.

2 pounds fresh swordfish
4 fresh rosemary branches for
   skewers or bamboo skewers
1 recipe ginger marinade (optional)
sprinkle of salt and white pepper

Ginger Marinade:
2 tablespoons grated ginger
1 tablespoon dijon mustard
1 teaspoon garlic, finely chopped
1 teaspoon IGA sugar
1/4 cup good wine vinegar
1/2 cup olive oil
1 teaspoon salt
1/2 teaspoon white pepper

If you are using fresh rosemary skewers, take a firm hold of a bushy straight branch and pull the leaves off the branch, leaving a wooden skewer.

If you are using wooden skewers, soak them in water for ten minutes before threading your fish onto them so they won't burn on the BBQ or under the broiler.

Cut the swordfish steaks into nice sized chunks about 1 "x 1". Thread them onto the skewers and marinate them, if you wish. Cook over coals or under the broiler for 3 minutes on each side, being careful not to overcook.

Serve with other grill vegetables over pillows of steamed rice. Swordfish is excellent when marinated. An hour is all it takes to absorb nice flavors, but can marinate for up to four hours.

If you use rosemary skewers, the herb flavor permeates the fish nicely and doesn't necessarily need marinating.

To prepare marinade simply whisk together all ingredients. Marinate the brochettes for up to four hours. This marinade also works beautifully with prawns, scallops, or any other firm fleshed fish.

This recipe will marinate about two pounds of seafood. Serves: 4

Scaloppine Alla Marsala

1 pound thin veal cutlets
1 sliced lemon (sliced thin)
1/2 cup flour
1/2 cup marsala (sweet or dry)
1/2 pound Crystal butter
Schilling garlic salt and pepper (to
   taste)
1/2 sliced mushrooms
1/4 cup lemon juice

Kay Albiani
Elk Grove, CA

Have veal flattened and cut into 4-inch pieces. Roll veal in flour, heat skillet; Melt butter, brown cutlets quickly. Add mushrooms, lemon juice and marsala Wine, Cover. Simmer over low flame about 5 minutes or until meal is tender. Serve hot with fresh lemon slices. If you like sweeter taste, use sweet marsala, for tartar taste use dry marsala. Serves: 4

Steak Chicana

Ruben Ramirez-Cafe Delicias

Ruben Ramirez opened Cafe Delicias in Auburn in 1970. Managing three other locations - Roseville, Rocklin and Granite Bay Shopping Center. Uses same methods that father used when he began business in 1960.

1 pound beef
1/2 tomato
green pepper
onions
black pepper, to taste
garlic, to taste
Schilling cumin, to taste
6-8 ounces green chilis
water

Cut steak into strips. Saute beef, tomato, green pepper and onions with black pepper, garlic and cumin. Blend green chilis. Add to beef mixture. Add enough water just to cover beef. Simmer for a few minutes.

Thai Green Curry With Chicken

Mai Pham

Lemon Grass Cafe

Lemon Grass Restaurant

Recognized as one the nation's preeminent Vietnamese restaurateur and chef, Mai Pham has dazzled Sacramento since she first opened Lemon Grass Restaurant in 1988. Her second restaurant, Lemon Grass Cafe, builds on the strengths of the original concept but emphasizes on fun, healthy food and casual dining.

1 1/2 cups sliced bamboo shoots*
1/2 cup unsweetened coconut milk*
2 cups chicken stock
1 tablespoon Thai-style green curry*
3 tablespoons IGA sugar
1 tablespoon fish sauce
1 1/2 pounds chicken breast, sliced 1/4 " thin
1 stalk lemon grass, cut into 2-inch pieces, bruised lightly
    with back of knife*
4 frozen kaffir lime leaves, cut into thin slivers*
1/2 cup peas
15 Thai basil leaves, cut into half
sprigs of cilantro for garnish
salt to taste

Bring a small pot of water to a full boil and then add bamboo shoots. Let boil for five minutes. Then drain and rinse in cold water. Strain and set aside. In a nonstick fry pan, heat half of the coconut milk then add curry paste and lemon grass. Let mixture sizzle and give off a wonderful fragrance. Add chicken stock, lime leaves, fish sauce and sugar. Bring to a boil. Add chicken and cook for 5-7 minutes, or until the chicken turns white.

Add remaining coconut milk, bamboo shoots and peas. Continue to simmer until vegetables are thoroughly hot, about 2-3 minutes. Do not allow coconut milk to boil as it will separate. Remove from heat. Add fresh basil just before serving. Garnish with cilantro and serve immediately with steamed jasmine rice. Serves: 3-4 with other dishes

*Available at most Asian grocery stores

Breaded Chicken

Mike Morello

Born and raised in the San Francisco Bay area, worked for South San Francisco Police Department for 14 years. Lived in Auburn for last 15 years, Presently Chief of Auburn Police Dept. Wife's name Sue, 2 daughters, 1 granddaughter. Recipe is a family recipe.

4 skinless, boneless chicken breasts
.2 tablespoons
Crystal milk
2 IGA California eggs
1/2 cup flour
1 cup bread crumbs
1/4 cup Kraft Parmesan cheese
1/2 teaspoon pepper
1/2 teaspoon salt
1/2 teaspoon Schilling garlic powder
sprinkle Schilling parsley
1 small can of mushrooms

Make a batter of milk and eggs (2 eggs at a time). Make a bread crumb mixture adding cheese, pepper, salt garlic powder and parsley. Tenderize fillets. Dip each fillet in batter then in flour then back in batter then coat with bread crumb mix. Fry in oil until brown, place in baking pan pour contents of mushroom can including water, cover with foil and cook 30 minutes at 350° in oven. Serves: 4

Capellini Pollo

Julie and Greg Virga

Virga's Restaurant and Bar
Anything Goes!

The Virgas co-own an Italian restaurant. Lending a regular noontime presence is their father, Judge Mike Virga. In fact, the Superior Court judge has enjoyed so many lunches there that Table 40 bears a plaque with his name. Recently, the Virgas branched out, opening a side business called "Anything Goes, Catering by Virga's." Among their clients: Governor Pete Wilson and Assembly Speaker Willie Brown. Chef Rick Handy changes the menu twice a year, but hand-stuffed raviolli and risotto are enduring favorites.

2 grilled chicken breasts, sliced into bite-sized pieces
1/4 cup sun-dried tomatoes
1/8 cup fresh basil - coarsely chopped
1 tablespoon minced garlic (approximately 3 cloves)
4 tablespoons Parmesan cheese
2 tablespoons toasted pine nuts
1/4 cup balsamic vinegar (or to taste)
1/2 cup olive oil
16 ounces capellini pasta

Grill chicken breast until slightly under-cooked, slice into bite-sized pieces and set aside. Coarsely chop sun-dried tomatoes and set aside. Coarsely chop basil, set aside. Lightly toast pine nuts in a saute pan (3 or 4 minutes). Cook off capellini pasta according to directions on package.

Saute garlic in olive oil about 5 minutes or until garlic becomes clear. Add grilled chicken breast pieces and sun-dried tomatoes and continue to saute for about 7 minutes. Deglaze with balsamic vinegar (remember this is to taste - you may want to add a little more or a little less than a 1/4 cup) Toss with cooked pasta and fresh basil. Salt and pepper to taste.

Garnish with Parmesan cheese and toasted pine nuts. Serves: 4

Raisin Sauce

Dennis Haworth

This recipe was my mother's. It is a favorite of our family and are asked for it continually. Wonderful on Ham or Pork.

1 cup IGA brown sugar, packed
1/2 cup hot water
1/2 cup seedless raisins (to taste)
1/4 cup cider vinegar
2 tablespoons Crystal butter
1 1/2 teaspoons Worcestershire
   sauce
1/2 teaspoon salt
1/8 teaspoon pepper
1 cup currant jelly
2 tablespoons cornstarch

Mix brown sugar and cornstarch, slowly stir in vinegar and water. Simmer together 5 minutes stirring until sugar is dissolved. Add rest of ingredients and cook until jelly is dissolved. Serve hot over ham or pork

Chicken Enchilada Verde

12 ounces verde (green) enchilada
   sauce
3 corn tortillas
3 cups shredded chicken
3 cups grated Kraft mozzarella or
   Kraft Monterey Jack cheese
sliced olives (optional)
Crystal sour cream

Cover bottom of round casserole dish with verde sauce. Layer 2 tortillas, chicken, 2/3 cheese and 2/3 sauce. Top with tortilla, remaining cheese and sauce. Cover and microwave on high for 5 minutes or until cheese is well melted. Let stand covered for 5 minutes. Garnish with sliced olives and sour cream. Then serve. Accompany with Spanish rice and refried beans.
Serves: 4

Stephanie Cahill
Galt, CA

Crab Cioppino Siciliana

1/4 cup olive oil
2 cloves garlic
1 cup Schilling parsley
3 pounds squid
1 pound scallops
1/2 pound prawns
3 large cans tomato sauce
4 medium crabs
4 pounds clams

Heat oil in large 8-10 quart pan, saute diced onions, garlic and parsley for 2-3 minutes. Add cleaned squid, scallops and prawns until slightly browned, about 5 minutes. Add 3 large cans of tomato sauce, keep on medium heat for 20 minutes, stir frequently. Add cracked and cleaned crab, stir in, add clams, cook on medium heat about twenty minutes or until clam shells have opened up. Serves: 10-12

Vera Girolami
Modesto, CA

Salmon With Fennel Flavored Potato
And The Essence Of Ginger Hollandaise

Linda Ferrari

Linda has 6 children, a catering business, teaches cooking classes and has published cookbooks. This makes a beautiful first course. It looks like a lot of work but it takes only 20 minutes to prepare You can fix the salmon early in the day wrap in foil and refrigerate until ready to cook The potato could also be prepared ahead and warmed.

Salmon:
1/2 pound of salmon fillets
1 tablespoons Worcestershire sauce
4 lemon slices
2 teaspoons fresh fennel sprigs
1 teaspoon fresh dill
2 teaspoons ginger liqueur
pinch of salt and pepper

Potato:
1 large Idaho russet potato, peeled
    and diced
1 medium fennel bulb, chopped
1 clove garlic, slow cooked in 2
    tablespoons Crystal butter
3 tablespoons Crystal milk
salt and pepper to taste

Sauce:
3 IGA California egg yolks
2 teaspoons ginger liqueur
2 teaspoons
 fresh fennel sprigs
1/2 teaspoon dried tarragon
juice of 1/2 lemon
1/4 teaspoon white pepper
1/4 teaspoon salt
5 tablespoons Crystal butter, melted

Vegetables:
1 tablespoon carrot cut julienne
1 tablespoon chives cut in 1 inch
    pieces

Preheat oven to 375°. Put potato and fennel into a pan and cover with water. Cook until potato and fennel are tender.

Mash potato and fennel and add garlic-butter mixture, milk and salt and pepper to taste set aside. You can warm right before using.

Take a 12-inch piece of foil. Lay the salmon fillets skin side down on the foil. Lay the lemon slices on the fillets and then sprinkle the fillets with Worcestershire, fennel sprigs, dill, ginger, salt and pepper. Roll up sides and ends of foil to enclose salmon.

Put on a cookie sheet and cook in a preheated 375° oven until fish flakes. This takes about 15 minutes Remove from oven and remove lemon slices.

Cover carrot and chives with water and blanch. This can be done in the microwave in 2 minutes.

To make sauce put egg yolks, liqueur, fennel, tarragon, lemon juice, pepper and salt into a blender Blend a few times.

Right before serving melt butter and while hot add to eggs while machine is running.

To assemble, warm potatoes, if necessary, and then put into a decorating bag with a number 828 tip (if you do not have this you can just put a spoonful on but it is so pretty using the tip).

Pour some sauce on each plate. Then put a 3-inch piece of salmon on top of sauce (if you use a thin spatula to lift the salmon the skin will come off easily)

Now squeeze a pretty round of potato on top of the salmon, being careful not to cover the salmon completely. Sprinkle with the blanched vegetables and serve. Serves: 4

Stuffed Rack Of Lamb With A Cumberland Sauce

Ruth Johanson

The recipe is from Ruth's Scottish grandmother, Margaret Sloane Hislop. Ruth wrote for 11 years, under the title "Sierra Cooks" for Sierra Heritage Magazine. As writer and Food Editor of the foothill publication, it was her pleasure to judge the annual Tahoe Food and Wine Show.

2 7-rib Racks of Lamb

Stuffing:
6 slices crustless white or wheat bread (or a combination)
1 medium onion, finely chopped
1 cup finely chopped mushrooms, wrung in towel to dry
3/4 cube Crystal butter
2 teaspoons Schilling thyme
1 teaspoon salt
1/2 teaspoons pepper

Sauce:
1 orange
1 lemon
1 12-ounce jar red currant jelly
3 shallots
1/4 teaspoon Schilling cayenne pepper
1/4 teaspoon Schilling ginger
1/4 cup Port wine

To prepare stuffing: In a large bowl, gently shred bread and crumb by lightly rubbing between palms. Combine with Thyme, salt and pepper. Saute onions and mushrooms in butter until limp and golden.

Add mixture to bread crumbs, combining well. Additional Thyme, salt or pepper may be added to taste.

To prepare the lamb make a pocket in a 7-rib rack of lamb keeping your knife as close to the bones as possible. Put a generous amount of stuffing into the pocket and secure with small skewers, if necessary. Brush lamb with oil and dust with salt and pepper.

Repeat process of second rack.

Place lamb, fat side up, on a roasting pan. Roast in a preheated 450° oven for 10 minutes. Reduce oven temperature to 400° and roast for 15-20 minutes more, according to desire doneness.

Remove lamb from oven and let rest for about 10 minutes. Using a sharp knife, cut carefully between the bones, carving the rack into pieces two chops thick.

To prepare the sauce, canelle the peeling from the orange and lemon. Cut into 4-inch lengths. Mince shallots and place with peelings in a saucepan of water.

Boil for three minutes, then drain. Combine mixture with juice of the orange and 1/2 the lemon. Add remaining ingredients except Port, and simmer for 30 minutes. Stir in Port and heat through. Serves: 6

Sauteed Calamari Piccata

Shannon's Lakeside Grill

4 cups sliced mushrooms
2-3 ounces capers
1/2 cup white wine
2 tablespoons fresh lemon juice
4 cups Crystal heavy cream
1/2 cup garlic butter
IGA California eggs, Crystal milk,
    flour, chopped parsley

Take sliced mushrooms, capers, white wine, fresh lemon juice, then reduce this in sauce pan until almost dry. Then add heavy cream, reduce by half. Remove from the heat and stir in garlic butter. In a separate dish mix together 4 eggs and 2 cups of milk. Mix well. Have another separate dish of all purpose flour available. Take calamari steak (unfrozen) and dip into egg wash, dredge calamari into flour and saute until light golden brown. Pour piccata sauce over completed calamari steak. Garnish with lemons and chopped parsley. Enjoy! Can be enjoyed over linguini also! Serves: 10

Sauce for Salmon

1/2 cup Poupon dijon mustard
2 tablespoons dry Schilling mustard
2-4 tablespoons IGA sugar
1/4 cup white nice vinegar
2/3 cup Wesson oil
2/3 cup chopped fresh dill or 1-2
    tablespoons dry dill to taste.

Bev Williams
Penn Valley, CA

Combine all ingredients and whisk thoroughly. Refrigerate. Will keep for 6 weeks.

London Broil

John Reinking

John Reinking is presently serving as the Placer County Superintendent of Schools. Mr. Reinking and his wife Jean live in Newcastle.

Tenderized flank steak (run through tenderizer twice)
Bacon strips

Marinade Sauce:
1/8 cup soy sauce
1/4 cup Wesson oil
1/4 teaspoon dry Schilling ginger
2 cloves garlic (pressed)
1/2 cup red wine (Burgundy or sweet)

Place two strips of bacon on flank steak. Roll steak and bacon. Cut into slices approximately 1 to 1-1/2 inches thick. Use wooden skewers to secure meat. Marinate meat in sauce overnight. Grill meat on BBQ between 5-8 minutes on each side (length of time depends on temperature of grill). Serves: 6-8

Grilled Swordfish

1 large tomato, diced
1/2 cup marinated artichoke hearts, torn
2 tablespoons frozen corn
1 green onion, thinly sliced
4 swordfish steaks (1-inch thick)
2 lemons

Mix first 4 ingredients, set aside. Squeeze juice of 1 lemon over steaks. Grill 4-6 inches from flame for 5-6 minutes. Turn and squeeze juice of second lemon over steaks and grill for 5-6 minutes. Just prior to fish being served, spread tomato, etc... over fish and let stand on grill 2 to 3 minutes. Serves: 4

Kristen Swansen
Sacramento, CA

Madeira Chicken

Suzanne Buchholz

My summers as a youth were spent cooking for crews of men who were branding cattle or baling hay on the family ranch in the Midwest. Now I cook for my family and friends-nothing fancy, just plain, good food. This recipe for Madeira Chicken was developed from a gourmet dish. It's a simpler version which is better suited to the tastes of my family and guests.

16-20 pieces of chicken on the bone
salt and pepper
2 tablespoons Crystal butter or Kraft margarine
2-3 tablespoons vegetable oil
16-20 whole mushrooms
1 10-ounce bag frozen pearl onions, thawed and drained
2 tablespoons IGA sugar
4 cloves garlic, crushed
1 cup beef broth
1/2 cup red wine vinegar
1/2 cup Madeira wine
1 teaspoon dried tarragon
1 teaspoon dried Schilling thyme
4 teaspoons tomato paste
1 package brown gravy mix
parsley for garnish

Salt and pepper chicken pieces in oil and margarine. Saute a few at a time until brown on all sides. Remove to casserole dish. Saute whole mushrooms in same pan until lightly browned. Remove and add to chicken. Add onions to saucepan, sprinkle with sugar, and saute over moderate heat, stirring until glazed and lightly browned.

Stir in garlic, beef broth, vinegar, Madeira, tarragon, thyme, tomato paste, and brown gravy mix. Bring to a boil, stirring constantly. Pour sauce and any brown bits that stick to the bottom of the pan over chicken and mushrooms in casserole. Cover and bake at 350° for 45 minutes.

With slotted spoon, remove chicken, onions, and mushrooms to serving platter. Spoon over desired amount of sauce. Garnish with parsley. May be refrigerated up to 2 days or frozen after baking.

Potato Burgers

1 pound ground beef
1 medium Idaho potato - grated
1/2 small onion - grated
1 can cream of chicken soup
1/2 soup can of water
Salt & pepper to taste

Pam King

Combine soup and water, mix well and set aside. Combine ground beef, potato, onion, slat and pepper. Make out into 1-inch thick patties. Brown patties in 2 tablespoons oil, do not cook through, drain on paper towels. Remove excess grease from skillet leaving all bits and pieces. Arrange patties in skillet, pour soup over cover. Simmer 25-30 minutes.

California Sturgeon
With Garlic Mashed Potatoes And Arugula Pesto

Dave Kemplin-Scott's Seafood Grill and Bar

Dave Kemplin is a chef at Scott's Seafood Grill & Bar, who is committed to the light clean flavors of the nineties. This dish displays American Regional and California Cuisine, combining local farm-raised Sturgeon with a hearty "homeland" favorite of garlic mashed potatoes and California-grown arugula pesto.

4 7-ounce servings sturgeon filets

Garlic Mashed Potatoes:
1 1/2 pounds Idaho russet potatoes, boiled or steamed
2 tablespoons Crystal butter
3 tablespoons roasted garlic puree
1/8 cup Crystal half & half
1/4 cup Crystal sour cream
2 tablespoons chopped chives
salt & white pepper to taste

Arugula Pesto:
1/2 bunch arugula
1/2 bunch basil
1 clove garlic
1/2 tablespoon pine nuts
pinch of salt

To prepare potatoes, smash all ingredients together and keep hot.

For pesto: in food processor add all ingredients and puree.

Slowly pour in 1 cup olive oil.

Char-grill Sturgeon 3 minutes on each side or until desired doneness.

Place on garlic mashed potatoes and top with arugula pesto. Serves: 4

Shepherd Lamb or Veal Shanks

Phyllis Grupe

Cooking is a passion for our whole family. Meals are family time with preparation and clean up duties shared. I try to keep my cooking style healthy, speedy and tasty. I use as many short cuts as possible, but always keep in mind the importance of quality, fresh ingredients, with as few additives and preservatives as possible.

4-6 lean, split lamb or veal shanks (about 3 pounds)
1 1/2 cups strong coffee
1 cup bourbon

Brown shanks in olive oil over medium heat for 5 minutes. Pour off an excess fat. Place in Dutch oven. Add coffee and Bourbon. Cover tightly with foil or lid (no peeking). Bake at 275° all day. Salt and pepper to taste. Serve with baby carrots, petite peas and rice or risotto or pasta or mashed potatoes or roasted potatoes. It is yummy and Oh so easy! Serves: 4-6

Betsy's Clarendon House Chicken With Apples

6 chicken thighs or split breasts
6 celery
1 cup carrots, peeled baby carrots
2 red delicious apples, peeled and sliced
1 medium onion, chopped
1 cup apple cider
1/2 teaspoon salt
1/2 teaspoon white pepper
1/2 cup heavy Crystal whipping cream

Betsy Groves
Old Sacramento, CA

Brown chicken, skin side down (no oil). Add remaining ingredients, simmer 30 minutes then stir in whipping cream. Subtle apple flavor but really tasty. Serves: 4-6

Salmon Croquettes

1 can of Salmon
1 IGA California egg
1/3 cup onion (diced)
1/3 cup celery (diced)
1/3 cup Kraft cheddar cheese (diced)
salt
pepper
2 cups crackers (crushed)
Wesson oil

Demetrice P. Cheathon
Sacramento, CA

Mix salmon, egg, onion, celery, cheese, salt and pepper in a large bowl. Form into six patties. Coat each patty in cracker crumbs. Fry in oil until golden brown. Serve right away. Makes six croquettes. Serves: 3

Korean Beef Skewers

2 tablespoons Wesson oil
3/8 cup soy sauce
3 tablespoons IGA brown sugar
2 garlic cloves, crushed
1/4 teaspoon monosodium
    glutamate
2 tablespoons wine, white
dash pepper
2 tablespoons sesame seeds,
    toasted & ground
3 pounds flank steak, slightly frozen
bamboo skewers

Matt Chan
Sacramento, CA

Wipe steak with damp paper towels. Trim off excess fat. Cut steak lengthwise, wrap separately with plastic wrap and freeze slightly. Slice each half, across the grain, at 45° angle in very thin slices, no more than 1/4 inch thick.

Mix all the sauce ingredients. Mix the sliced meat with the sauce and let sit covered in the refrigerator for 3/4 to 2 hours. Then soak bamboo skewers in water for at least 30 minutes.

Thread each strip of steak on a skewer. Then grill over a very hot fire 1 to 2 minutes per side. Serve immediately. Serves: 6

Dingus McGee's Famous Flank Steak

Bob Townsend

Dingus McGee's Restaurant

Bob has been co-owner of Dingus McGee's Restaurant for 20 years. He focuses his attention on providing a comfortable, interesting atmosphere for locals and travelers alike. The food is regional American cooking and the well-trained staff is always accommodating.

Marinade:
1 quart soy sauce
1 quart red wine vinegar
3/4 pound IGA brown sugar
1/3 cup granulated garlic
1 ground up ginger root, about 1/3 cup

Sauce:
1/3 of marinade
equal amount of pineapple juice
1 lemon
1 orange
1/8 pound Crystal butter
cornstarch

Purchase flank steaks from grocer, lay out and cut in 8-ounce servings. Marinate for 4-12 hours. The marinade portions here will serve approximately 8 people. The marinade will hold in the refrigerator, but proportions can be adjusted to desire.

Mix marinade with pineapple juice. Cut orange and lemon in half and squeeze juice into sauce. Put peels into sauce also. Bring to a boil. Discard lemon and orange peels. Thicken with cornstarch and strain into a container. Mix in butter.

Slice steak thinly across grain at 45° angle and fan out on a dinner plate. Drizzle some sauce over steak and serve with a ramekin of sauce on the side. Serve with rice and vegetables.

California Crab Burgers

4 hamburger buns, split
1 can crab meat, drained very dry
1/4 cup celery, chopped fine
1/2 cup grated Kraft cheddar
    cheese
2 tablespoons finely chopped onion
1/2 cup Kraft mayonnaise
3 or 4 dashes tabasco sauce
salt & pepper to taste

Edna Betti
Escalon, CA

Mix together well, spread on buns. Broil until cheese is melted and tops are slightly brown. By keeping a couple of cans of crab meat in the pantry, and hamburger buns in the freezer, one is always prepared for those emergency situations which face each of us occasionally.

Bechamel-Coated Fried Chicken

3 cups chicken stock or canned
    chicken broth
4 halved, boneless, skinless chicken
    breasts (1 1/2 pounds)

Bechamel Coating:
5 tablespoons Crystal butter
6 tablespoons white wheat flour
3/4 cup Crystal milk
1/4 teaspoon Schilling thyme
salt
ground white pepper
3 quarts olive oil
1 IGA California egg, beaten with 2
    tablespoons water
1 cup dried bread crumbs

Jeni Rose
Sacramento, CA

A novel method for keeping fried chicken non-greasy. The Bechamel coating forms a protective layer that helps keep the meat extra moist. It is important to chill the coated chicken until the bechamel is firm. For an hors d'oeuvre, use the technique described in this recipe, but substitute bite-sized pieces of chicken.

Bring chicken stock to boil in a large saucepan. Add chicken breasts; return stock to boil, cover, and simmer until chicken is cooked through, about 12 minutes. Remove chicken breast; reserve 3/4 cup of the chicken stock for the Bechamel coating. Cool chicken breasts to room temperature.

Meanwhile, heat butter in a small saucepan. Add flour; cook over low heat, stirring constantly until flour is incorporated into the butter, about 30 seconds. Continuing to stir constantly, gradually add milk and reserved 3/4 cup chicken stock. Simmer, still stirring constantly, until Bechamel thickens, about 2 minutes. Stir in thyme and seasonings with 1/4 teaspoon salt and 1/8 teaspoon white pepper or to taste; cool to room temperature.

Dip each chicken breast in this bechamel, then refrigerate until Bechamel is firm, about 1 hour. (Can be refrigerated overnight.)

Heat oil in a Dutch oven or electric deep fryer to 365°. Dip both sides of each chicken breast into the egg-water mixture, then dredge in bread crumbs. Fry chicken breasts, turning once, until golden brown, about 5 minutes. Drain chicken breasts on paper towels and serve. Serves: 4

Main Dishes

Beth's Ham

baking ham with bone
1 can pineapple slices
whole cloves
1/4 cup IGA brown sugar
orange juice
drippings make nice, sweet gravy

Preheat oven to 350°. Place ham in glass baking dish. "Decorate" with pineapple using cloves to hold slices in place. Combine juice from canned pineapple brown sugar and enough orange juice to make 2 cups liquid. Pour about 1 cup over ham, save rest to pour later. Bake uncovered at 350°, 20 minutes per pound.

Beth Ruyak

Beth Ruyak co-anchors "News 10 at 6:00" and "News 10 at 11:00" weeknights. Ruyak has considerable national experience including "USA Today", "Good Morning America," " The Home Show", the 1992 Summer Olympics and the 1994 Winter Olympics. She joined KXTV in August, 1992.

Newsten Noodle Bake

1 pound ground beef
1 can tomato sauce (15-ounce)
1 cup Crystal sour cream (low fat if you prefer)
1 cup Crystal cottage cheese (low fat if you prefer)
1 onion, chopped
8 ounces wide egg noodles
grated cheese
seasoning to taste

Brown meat, add tomato sauce and seasonings and simmer 15-20 minutes. Add other ingredients to cooked noodles. Layer in casserole. Top with cheese. Bake 30-45 minutes at 350°.

Jennifer Smith

Jennifer Smith has been with KXTV since July 1980. She co-anchors NEWS 10 AT NOON and NEWS 10 AT 5:00. Smith graduated with honors from Lynchburg College in Virginia with a degree in Political Science and International Relations. Smith has been honored as Young Career Woman and Woman of the Year by area business and professional clubs.

Busy Day Casserole

In a large skillet brown and chop into pieces:

1 pound ground round beef

drain off extra grease and add:

1 cup chopped onions
1/2 cup chopped green bell peppers
1 (8-ounce) can mushrooms, sliced and drained
2 cups chopped fresh or canned tomatoes
1/2 cup uncooked rice
1 teaspoon Schilling chili powder
Salt and pepper to your taste

Bring to a boil. Transfer to a greased 1 1/2 quart casserole. Cover and bake in a 350° oven for 40 minutes. Serves: 6

Mrs. Edwinn Butterman
Lodi, CA

Mom's Beef Stroganoff

1 1/2 pounds round sirloin or chuck steak, cubed
flour
2 tablespoons shortening
2 onions, chopped
1 clove garlic, minced
1 cup sliced mushrooms
2 cans beef broth
1 cup Crystal sour cream
2 teaspoons Worcestershire sauce
6 drops tabasco
salt and pepper to taste
cooked egg noodles or rice

Brown flour-coated meat and add onions, garlic and mushrooms. Cook slowly for 5 minutes. Combine remaining ingredients and pour over meat. Cover and simmer for 1 hour or until tender. Serve over noodles or rice. Serves: 6

Lisa Lundquist
Stockton, CA

Tijuana Torte

1 pound ground turkey
1 medium onion, chopped
1 pound can stewed tomatoes
1 (8-ounce) tomato sauce
1 package taco seasoning
flour tortillas
1 pound grated Kraft cheddar
   cheese
1 (4-ounce) can diced chilies
1 1/2 cups Crystal sour cream

Theresa Kentrote
Carmichael, CA

Brown onion in a little pan and add ground turkey. Add other ingredients except cheddar cheese and sour cream. Place 1/4 cup mixture in a 9x13-inch baking dish. Place a layer of tortillas on top. Add more mixture and add 1 1/2 cups of sour cream and then the grated cheese. Bake at 350° for 25 minutes, until cheese is bubbly. Serves: 6

Tuna Casserole

1 bag of egg noodles
3 cans mushroom soup
3 cans tuna
1 can peas
1/2 sliced onion
1 bag of potato chips
1 cup of sliced Kraft cheddar cheese

Chuck Bolkcom
Sacramento, CA

Pre-Heat oven at 325°. Boil noodles. Mix soup, tuna, peas (after draining water), onion, and cheese into large casserole pan or roaster. Stir in noodles. Layer potato chips and extra cheese on top of mixed casserole and place pan in oven, uncovered for 20 to 25 minutes. Serve hot. Serves: any large family

A Meal In A Casserole

Father Dan Madigan

Born in Limerick County, Ireland. Came to United States in 1966. Presently Pastor of St. Joseph's Church, Clarksburg. Founded Sacramento Food Bank Services in 1976 and is still its Director.

2 or 3 large Idaho potatoes, quartered and sliced thin
1 medium onion, sliced and quartered
1 16-ounce can creamed corn
1 pound pork sausage
1 16-ounce can stewed tomatoes

In large covered casserole: layer potatoes, onions, salt and pepper to taste. Pour creamed corn over potatoes and onions. Crumble pork sausage over corn.

Pour tomatoes over all. Cover. Bake at 350° for 1 hour, or until potatoes are tender. Serves: 6

Lasagna

8 ounces lasagna noodles, cooked
1/2 pound Italian sausage
1 pound ground beef
1 cup onion, chopped
2 cloves garlic, minced
1 (28-ounce) can tomatoes, cut up, undrained
2-6 cans tomato paste
2 teaspoons sugar
2 teaspoons salt
1 1/2 teaspoons basil leaves
1/2 teaspoon fennel seed
1/4 teaspoon pepper
1 (15-ounce) container Kraft Ricotta cheese
1 IGA California egg, beaten
1 tablespoon Schilling parsley flakes
1/2 teaspoon salt
4 cups (1 pound) shredded Kraft mozzarella cheese
3/4 cup grated Kraft Fresh Parmesan cheese

Brown sausage, ground beef, onion and garlic; drain.

Add next seven ingredients. Bring to a boil.

Reduce heat, simmer for 20 minutes.

In medium bowl, blend Ricotta, egg, parsley and salt.

Spoon 1 1/2 cups meat sauce into 9x13-inch baking dish. Layer 1/3 each lasagna, remaining meat sauce, Ricotta mix, mozzarella and Parmesan. Repeat layers.

Cover. Bake at 375° for 25 minutes. Uncover, bake 20 minutes more.

Mitch Richmond

Mitch Richmond has accomplished 6 seasons in professional basketball. He and wife Juli have a 1-year old son, Mitchell Phillip. He earned bachelor's degree in social sciences from KSU. Established "Solid As A Rock" Foundation, a college scholarship fund for high school student athletes in his hometown of Fort Lauderdale. Was given the "Special Friend Award" by the National committee to Prevent Child Abuse for his nationally televised PSA on the cause. Spokesperson for the Bank of America Scholar-Athlete Program in the Sacramento area. He plays for the Sacramento Kings.

Rice and Cheese Casserole

1 cup white long grain rice
1 teaspoon Crystal butter
1/4 teaspoon onion powder
1/4 teaspoon Schilling garlic powder
3/4 cup grated Kraft cheddar cheese
1/2 cup grated carrots
1/2 tablespoon Schilling parsley flakes

Cook rice until tender. Add butter and spices. Stir in 1/4 cup cheese, carrots and parsley, mix well. Put into baking dish and sprinkle top with remaining cheese. Bake at 400° for 20-25 minutes.

Diana Hawkins
Sacramento, CA

Char's Homemade Enchiladas

Charlotte Hernandez

Charlotte Hernandez is with the Placer County Office of Education/Child Care Services.

6 boneless chicken breasts
1 tablespoon salt
1 tablespoon Schilling garlic powder
1 teaspoon cumino
1 teaspoon pepper
1 cup diced olives
2 cups cheese
6 green onions
24 corn tortillas

Sauce:
1 tablespoon olive oil
1 tablespoon Schilling garlic powder
1 tablespoon onion powder
1 tablespoon cumino
4 tablespoons flour
2 tablespoons Schilling chili powder
4 cups chicken broth

Steam chicken, let cool and shred by hand. Flavor chicken with salt, garlic powder, pepper, cumino and set aside.

To prepare sauce, saute garlic, onion powder, cumino, flour in olive oil. Slowly pour four cups chicken broth to sauteed ingredient and simmer for about 20 minutes. Chop green onions, olives and shred cheese.

Microwave your corn tortilla until soft. Dip tortilla into sauce and fill with olives, onions, chicken, and cheese, roll and set onto cooking dish.

Pour leftover sauce over enchiladas and bake 40 minutes at 350°. Serves: 10 to 12

Hot Chicken Salad

Julie Stringham

Julie Stringham is an avid community volunteer. She is President of the Board of Directors of the Child Abuse Prevention Council of Placer County. Julie was honored with an award from the California Department of Social Services for her good work on behalf of Placer County's abused and neglected children.

2 cups cooked chicken cut up
1 tablespoon grated onions
1 can sliced mushrooms
1/2 cup Kraft mayonnaise
2 cups sliced celery
1 can water chestnuts, sliced
2 tablespoons lemon juice
1/2 cup Crystal sour cream
grated Kraft cheddar cheese
bread crumbs

Combine chicken, onions, mushrooms, mayonnaise, celery, water chestnuts, lemon juice and sour cream.

Put in oiled 9x13-inch pan. Sprinkle with cheddar cheese and bread crumbs. Bake at 400° for 10 minutes or until bubbly.

Prawns Scorpio

Al Ricci

I'm a native of Sacramento who has always been interested in food preparation. This recipe was developed at Ricci's restaurant about three years ago when we decided to add fresh, fresh selections for our daily specials.

24 prawns
1 teaspoon chopped garlic
4 ounces Feta cheese
fresh basil (to taste)
dry Italian seasonings (to taste)
3 ounces Ouzo or Anisette
marinara sauce (meatless)
angel hair pasta
chopped parsley

Saute prawns in large skillet with virgin oil olive until prawns are light pink. Add garlic, fresh basil and Italian seasonings. Pour approximately 3 ounces of Ouzo or Anisette into skillet to flame prawns. Reduce heat after flame goes out and add 6 ounces of marinara sauce. Cover for approximately 2 minutes. Place prawns over angel hair pasta and spoon on sauce from skillet. Sprinkle 1 ounce of Feta cheese and chopped parsley over pasta and prawns then serve. Serves: 4

Okra Gumbo

4 cups fresh or frozen okra
1 (16-ounce) can of corn
4 cups stewed tomatoes or fresh
    garden tomatoes peeled with
    juices
1 medium yellow onion
3 stalks of chopped celery
2 pounds ground beef
2 pounds smoked sausage
1 pound bacon
2 pounds shrimp (optional)
1 teaspoon pepper
1/2 teaspoon creole seasonings
2 tablespoons Wesson oil
1 cup water

Nora E. Clipper
Stockton , CA

Bake bacon until crispy. Saute onions and celery in 2 tablespoons of oil. Add okra, cook until tender. Cook ground meat and drain fat. Return ground meat back to pan adding seasonings, vegetables, crumbled bacon and sliced 1/2" smoked sausage. Add 1 cup of water and let simmer for 3 minutes Serve over rice. Serves: 6-8

Marge's Ski Casserole

1 pound ground meat
1 cup rice (raw)
2 medium cans chopped ripe olives
1/2 teaspoon Schilling garlic powder
1/2 teaspoon dry Schilling parsley
1/2 teaspoon dry dill
1/4 cup pimento
1 can consomme
1/2 cup water
1 cup red wine
1 teaspoon salt
1/8 teaspoon pepper

Brown meat until no longer pink throw in the rest, stir. Cover and bake at 350° for 1 hour. Serves: 6-8

Mary Anne Conys
Stockton, CA

Casserole Italiano

1 pound ground beef
1/3 cup chopped onion
1 medium clove garlic, minced
1/2 -1 teaspoon Schilling oregano
1/2 teaspoon salt
1 can condensed tomato soup
2 cups cooked wide noodles
1 cup (4-ounce) shredded process
   cheese

Brown beef with onion, garlic, and seasonings. Stir to separate meat. Combine in 1 1/2 quart casserole with soup, 1/3 cup water, and noodles. Place cheese edge of casserole. Bake at 350° for 30 minutes. Serves: 4

Barbara Ann Forman
W. Sacramento, CA

Chili

3 pounds premium, extra lean, ground beef (cook meat
   first)
2 packages of Texas Chili (leave out the package of
   white sauce)
block of chili con carne
2 cans of chili with beans
5 quarts of water

Simmer and add chopped jalapeno pepper per taste.
Serves: 12-15

Senator Robert Presley

Robert Presley has had a distinguished and varied career, first as a highly-decorated soldier of World War II, then in local law enforcement and most recently in the California State Senate.

129

Chili Relleno Casserole

1 pound Kraft cheddar cheese, grated
2 7-ounce cans whole, green chilis
1/2 pound Kraft Monterey Jack cheese, grated
3 IGA California eggs
2 tablespoons flour
1 large can evaporated milk
1/2 teaspoon salt

Marjorie Thurman

Line 9x13-inch casserole with chili peppers (slice and take out seeds, cut in slices). Cover with cheese and top with a layer of peppers. Beat eggs, flour, salt, and milk. Pour over casserole and bake 45 minutes at 350° (until custard sets).

Swiss Steak with Rice

2 pounds of Round Steak
2 teaspoons salt
dash of pepper
6 onions, sliced
1/4 cup Kraft margarine
1 cup rice
2 bay leaves
1 10-ounces can of tomato soup
1 can of water
1 #2 can of green beans, drained

Bea and Kalli Louis
Loomis, CA

Season meat and sprinkle with flour. Brown onions in margarine. Remove and brown meat. Place meat in casserole, add onions, uncooked rice, and bay leaves. Pour soup and water mixed over top. Cover. Simmer low for 1 hour. Arrange beans around meat. Cook 15 minutes. Serves: 6-8 people.

Salmon Casserole

1 cup Salmon (canned or cooked)
1 cup Crystal milk
1 cup bread crumbs (seasoned)
1 IGA California egg and 1 yolk
1 tablespoon chopped onion
1 tablespoon vinegar

Topping:
1 beaten IGA California egg white
1/2 cup Kraft mayonnaise

Nona Hamilton
Auburn, CA

Mix together all ingredients but topping. Beat egg white stiff, fold into mayonnaise. Put mixture in square pan, top with topping. Bake 350° for 45 minutes. Serves: 4

Mom's Chili

2-1/2 pounds lean, coarsely ground beef
1 large coarsely chopped yellow onion
1 large can chopped & peeled tomatoes (if season is
    right go for fresh)
2 packets chili mix
extra Schilling chili powder to taste OR fresh chili's to taste
    (if very spicy is your thing)
1-2 cans large, red kidney beans

Saute ground beef and onions together over medium heat until lightly browned. Add tomatoes, chili mix and chili powder/fresh chilis. Simmer over very low heat approximately one to one and one-half hours.

Refrigerate overnight, skim off fat. Reheat, add kidney beans and simmer until hot. Top with: chopped onions, grated sharp cheddar, *oyster crackers (*Tim insisted on these - wouldn't eat without).

Serve with: Rice, french-cut green beans, broccoli and **lime jello (**Tim tried to pass this off as a green vegetable. Lime Jello is good - especially if you want the grandchildren to eat)!

Timothy Busfield

Timothy Busfield is an all-American "Renaissance" man. Aside from his noteworthy film, TV and live stage career, Tim has cofounded two local award-winning theatres, The "B" Street Theatre and The Fantasy Theatre for Children. When he's not acting, directing or producing, he is pitching for the Smokey's, Sacramento's semi-pro ball team. Tim lives in Sacramento with his wife, Jennifer, and their three children. His favorite recipe is chili- thanks to his mom, Jean Blair, with her compliments and comments: None of the measurements are written in stone - play around.

Simmered Chinese Chicken

1 whole chicken fryer
    (approximately 3 pounds)
1 tablespoons Wesson oil
2 cloves garlic, crushed
1/3 cup soy sauce
1/3 cup packed IGA brown sugar
1/2 cup water
1 tablespoon catsup
1/4 cup dry sherry
1 green onion, sliced
1/4 teaspoon crushed red pepper
    (optional)
2 teaspoons toasted sesame seeds
    (optional)
    (place sesame seeds in flat
    pan - toast 10 minutes - 350°
    oven)
1 tablespoon cornstarch - 1/4 cup
    water (mix together)

Brown chicken in oil in Dutch oven. Mix together - soy sauce, brown sugar, 1/2 cup water, catsup, sherry, red pepper, garlic, and green onions.

Pour over chicken. Cover and simmer 35-45 minutes (depending on chicken size) until done.

Remove chicken to platter. Drain juices back into pan. Skim off fat and strain juices. Mix in cornstarch mixture. Cook - stirring constantly until thickened.

Carve and slice chicken. Place on serving platter. Spoon sauce over chicken. Sprinkle sesame seeds over sauce. Serves: 4

Eve Holden
Gold River, CA

Risotto Con Pollo

Tom Weatherby — Zoots

Chef Tom Weatherby has spent nearly 17 years in various restaurants in California. He has also travelled to over 25 countries studying the foods of the local area's. Tom was the chef for Spectum Foods, "Mac Arthur Park" in Palo Alto, California. Tom opened "Zoots" in 1992 in Rocklin and is planning to open a second restaurant next year. Zoots cuisine comes from the Northern part of Italy with some French and Austrian influences.

1 cup arborio rice or any short grain rice
4-5 cups chicken stock
1 ounce Crystal cream
1/2 cup mushrooms
1/4 cup onions
1/2 cup Kraft Parmesan cheese
4 ounces chopped chicken
flour
1 tablespoon Crystal butter
2 ounces white wine
2 cups mixed vegetables
1 ounce pine nuts (roasted)
chile peppers to taste
Wesson olive oil
salt and pepper to taste
chopped Italian parsley for garnish

Saute mushrooms and onions with a little oil on medium heat for 3 to 4 minutes. Add rice. Saute for 1 minute more. Add 2 cups of chicken stock and reduce heat to simmer. Add 2 more cups of chicken stock, one cup every 15 minutes. After rice is done remove from heat.

This can be done a day ahead of time.

In separate pan saute floured chicken until brown. Add vegetables for 1 minute on medium beat.

Deglaze pan with wine and add 2 to 4 ounces of chicken stock. Let mixture simmer until chicken is done and vegetables are to your liking. Add butter and cook until butter is melted.

In separate pan add risotto, 1/2 cup chicken stock and cream. Simmer until moisture is absorbed by the rice. Add cheese, mix quickly and remove from heat. Add salt and pepper to rice and vegetables to your taste. Rice should be creamy. Pour chicken mixture on risotto and garnish with parsley and serve.

Larcene's Chili Beans

Larcene Dixon

I am a retired teacher and very active in the community. I am a member of 2nd Baptist church, President of Church Women United A.A.U.W. and I am a recipient of the Susan B. Anthony Award.

1 Ham hock
2 cups red or pinto beans
1 1/2 pounds ground beef
1 can tomatoes
2 teaspoons Schilling chili powder
Seasoning salt
1/2 cup minced onions
Black pepper
1/4 cup minced garlic
Bay leaf
1 teaspoon sugar

Boil beans and ham hock, simmer for about 3 hours, until they are soft. Add bay leaf, garlic, onions, seasoning salt and black pepper.

Scramble beef in skillet. Pour beef in pot with beans. Add tomatoes, chili powder and sugar. Cover and let cook about 1 hour.

Mid-Eastern Chicken

Anne Rudin

Anne Rudin served for 12 years as a member of the Sacramento City Council, followed by nine years as mayor. She continues to be active in the community.

2 tablespoons lemon juice
2 whole chicken breasts, halved and boned
2 cloves garlic
1 teaspoon salt
1/4 teaspoon pepper freshly ground
1 tablespoon chopped fresh mint
1 teaspoon dried mint, crumbled
1 cup plain yogurt

Sprinkle lemon juice over chicken in glass baking dish. Marinate 10 minutes, turning once. Chop garlic with salt; mash to a paste. Combine with pepper, mint yogurt; mix well. Spread mixture over chicken and marinate 1 hour at room temperature. Arrange chicken on broiler pan, skin down. Place under broiler so that top of chicken is about 7" from heat. Broil 8-10 minutes on each side. Serves: 4

Chicana Italiano

Tom Pompei Jr.

A.K.A. Tower Tom "Mayor" of Lincoln Center - Stockton, CA

1/2 cup Crystal butter
2 tablespoons olive oil
3 cloves garlic
1 medium yellow onion
3 green chiles no seeds
1 teaspoon Schilling oregano and Schilling parsley
Salt and pepper to taste
2-3 small cans tomato sauce
1-1 1/2 pounds round steak tenderized (cut into small chunks or strips)

Chop onion, garlic, green chile.

Saute in butter or oil until soft. Add seasoning while saute in progress cook until onion is golden.

Prior to adding sauce add meat and saute until meat is no longer red. Add sauce. Cook low heat for 20 to 30 minutes or until sauce thickens to brownish red hue.

Serve over bed of white rice. Traditional Mexican dish with an Italian twist. Serves: 4

Chicken Paprika (Paprikash)

**Paul and Olga Kaut —
Czechoslavakian Restaurant**

Leaving Czechoslovakia in 1968 after Russian occupation, 1983 we settled down in Foothills in beautiful Meadow Vista, where we opened Czechoslovakian Restaurant where truly home-made Bohemian (Czech) food is served.

4 boneless, skinless chicken breast, or veal stew
1 large onion, chopped
6 tablespoons Crystal butter or Kraft margarine
1 tablespoon Hungarian paprika
2 cups water
2 tablespoons flour
1 cup Crystal sour cream
salt to taste

Dice the meat and sprinkle with salt. Fry onion in butter, add paprika and meat, and brown on all sides. Pour in water, cover and simmer until tender (about 30 minutes). Mix flour with sour cream. Add to gravy and simmer for 5 minutes. Serves: 4

Curried Rice Casserole

1 can cream of celery soup
1/2 teaspoon Schilling curry powder
1/2 cup chopped carrots
medium onion, chopped small
1 clove garlic, minced
1/2 cup chopped broccoli
1/2 cup chopped Chinese snow
    peas
1/2 cup chopped zucchini
4 cups cooked brown rice
1 cup Kraft sharp cheddar cheese,
    grated

*Yvonne Sinclair
Rocklin, CA*

Heat soup, cheese, and curry powder. Saute vegetables, onion, and garlic lightly. Mix all together with rice and place in buttered casserole. Heat until rice it hot all the way through. Serves: 8.

Italia Udon

**Sukayna Tourville
Tower Cafe**

4 ounces Udon*
4 ounces Sun-dried tomatoes
1/4 yellow onion
2 each green onion
3 tablespoons white wine
1 cup Crystal cream
1 tablespoon Wasabi paste*
4 ounces chicken breast (boneless, skinless)
1 each clove garlic (minced)
1 tablespoon Crystal butter
Pinch salt

Slice onion into thin strips, cut green onion into two inch lengths, slice chicken into this strips. Saute chicken with butter, garlic, sun-dried tomatoes, salt, and onion. When chicken is half cooked, add Wasabi, white wine, cream, then reduce the sauce until it coats a spoon. Add the cooked pasta to the pan and toss. Serve on a warm platter and garnish with cilantro leaves and strips of red bell pepper. Serves: 1
*Wasabi is a Japanese horseradish, Udon is an egg-less pasta and both are available in most Asian stores.

Chicken Casserole

2 cups diced cooked chicken
2 teaspoons finely chopped onion
1 cup sliced celery
1/2 cup sliced water chestnuts
1 1/2 cups cooked rice
1 tablespoon lemon juice
1/2 teaspoon salt
1/4 teaspoon pepper
3/4 cup Kraft mayonnaise
1/4 cup water

*Eloise McIntosh
Auburn, CA*

Combine chicken, onion, celery, water chestnuts, rice, lemon juice, salt and pepper.

Mix mayonnaise and water, add to chicken mixture. Turn into 9-inch square pan. Top with buttered bread crumbs. Bake at 450° until bubbly for 20-30 minutes.

I usually make 1 1/2 times recipe for 8-10 people.
Serves: 4-6

Chili

2 pounds ground chuck
2 packages Schilling chilli mix
1 29-ounce can pinto beans
1 27-ounce can kidney beans
1 28-ounce can whole tomatoes
2 cups catsup
5 cloves garlic
1 cube Crystal butter
1 cup water (more if desired)
1/2 cup molasses

*Pam Borgeson
Valley Springs, CA*

Fry the hamburger and chopped onions, adding the chilli mix at the end. Heat the beans and the tomatoes and all other ingredients. Add the hamburger mix and simmer for about 15 minutes

Blackbean Chili and Rice

1 can black beans
1 pound ground chuck
1 medium onion, chopped
2 cloves garlic, minced
1 (15-ounce) can chopped/peeled
    tomatoes (with juice)
1 can tomato soup, undiluted
1 tablespoon Schilling chili powder
1 teaspoon salt
1/2 teaspoon pepper

Celeste D. Malott
Stockton, CA

Brown ground chuck, minced garlic, and chopped onions. Add beans, tomatoes with juice, soup, chili powder, salt, and pepper.

Simmer 25-30 minutes uncovered. Serve on top of rice, polenta, or spoon bread. Garnish with grated cheddar cheese and heated salsa. Double recipe and freeze. Great leftover. Serves: 4-6

Chili Relleno Casserole

2 - 4 ounces cans whole green
    chilies
1 pound Kraft Monterey Jack cheese
2 IGA California eggs
2 cups Crystal milk
1 cup flour
2 teaspoons salt

Lucy Lainas
Sacramento, CA

Rinse and drain chilies. Slice cheese in thick slices. Layer chilies and cheese in a 2 quart casserole, making two layers of each. In another bowl, mix milk, flour and salt together, then add 2 whole eggs and mix well. Take this mixture and pour over cheese and chilies. Bake uncovered for 1 hour at 350°.

Turkey Scalopini

1 pound turkey breast
flour
Wesson cooking oil
1/2 pound mushrooms
1/2 cup of chicken broth
capers

R.V. Scheide

R.V. Scheide is the Arts Editor of the Sacramento News & Review. R.V. is an avid health fanatic and he commends Turkey Scalopini for those who are watching the fat in their diets.

Slice turkey into 1/4" thick medallions, then pound medallions flat with wood mallet. Dust with flour, then using a nonstick pan lightly coated with oil, fry over medium heat until edges turn white. Set aside, but keep warm.

Quarter mushrooms, place in pan, then add chicken broth. Remove mushrooms from sauce, add capers. Serves: 4

California Chili

California Tomato Growers Association

(A hot dish for a cold day)

1 pound ground beef
2 tablespoons Wesson oil
2 medium onions, chopped
1/2 cup green pepper, chopped
1 12-ounce can tomatoes
8 ounce can tomato sauce
10 1/2 ounce can tomato puree
2 bay leaves
2 teaspoons salt
1/4 teaspoon sugar
1 tablespoon Schilling chili powder
15 ounce can chili beans, or red
    kidney beans
dash of Schilling cayenne pepper

Brown beef well in oil in large skillet. Add all remaining ingredients except chili beans. Simmer 1 1/2 hours. If thicker chili is desired, simmer 2 1/2 hours. Add chili beans and heat. Serve hot.

French Enchiladas

1 tablespoon olive oil
1 whole red onion
2 cloves garlic
1 pound ground round steak
2 tablespoons Schilling cumin
    powder
1 (6-ounce) package Kraft sharp
    cheddar cheese
1 can pitted ripe olives
1 large can enchilada sauce
1 small can tomato sauce
1 bunch green onions
1 small can mushrooms in butter
12 corn tortillas
grated Kraft Parmesan cheese
salt and pepper to taste

John E. Cyr
Stockton, CA

Saute chopped onion and garlic in olive oil until brown. Add meat and saute salt and pepper and add cumin powder. Stir and brown thoroughly. Add sliced pitted olives. Cover and simmer.

Turn off heat and cover with grated cheddar cheese. Cover pan. Open can of enchilada sauce in open pot. Chop 3 or 4 green onions and add to sauce, also add can of mushrooms and can of tomatoes. Let simmer until boiling.

Turn down heat, dip corn tortilla in sauce. Take out and fold in meat mixture, roll in flat pan, cover with extra sauce. Sprinkle with more chopped onions.

Sprinkle with Parmesan cheese and serve. Serves: 4-6

Indonesian Grill And Rice

Sheila Anderson

Chicken:
1 cup teriyaki sauce
2 tablespoons olive oil
1/2 cup lime juice
1 clove minced garlic or to taste
1 teaspoon minced, fresh ginger or
   to taste
pinch fresh ground pepper
4 chicken breasts

Rice:
2 cups long grain white rice
4 cup chicken broth
1/2 cup white wine
3/4 teaspoons tumeric
1/2 teaspoon ginger

Mix first 5 ingredients. Pierce chicken, add it to the marinade and let stand for at least 3 hours.

Grill on outdoor barbeque and serve with Indonesian rice. Shrimp may be substituted for chicken and fresh vegetables may be added to marinade during the last 30 minutes and grilled with the chicken or shrimp.

For rice, mix all ingredients in a saucepan. Bring to a boil. Let simmer for 30 minutes.

Mound cooked rice in the center of a large platter. Surround it with grilled chicken (and vegetables if grilled) and garnish with edible flower blossoms.

Bonner Family Style Pastries

Edward Bonner

pastry dough
1 can stew beef - small cubes
Idaho potatoes, diced
carrots, sliced
salt and pepper

Amounts of ingredients vary according to your needs and tastes.

Roll enough dough to make approximately a 10-inch circle. Fill half the circle with small amounts of meat potatoes, carrots and onions.

Do not overfill. Salt and pepper to taste.

Dot with butter. Fold over pastry and seal edges. Make slits on top for vents. Place on cookie sheet.

Bake in oven 350° for 50-60 minutes.

Pastries can be made larger or smaller and cooking time varies

Veal Supreme

1 green pepper thinly sliced
1 onion thinly sliced
about 1 pound thinly sliced veal
    cutlet
1 can cream of chicken soup
1/4 cup white wine
flour
Crystal butter

Janet L. Berreth
Lodi, CA

Dip veal in flour. Brown well in butter about 10 minutes adding thinly sliced green pepper and onion rings the last few minutes. Stir in can cream of chicken soup, undiluted. Add 1/4 cup white wine. Cook covered 15 minutes or until veal is tender. Season to taste.

Green Enchiladas With Spicy Sauce

Judge Talmadge Jones

Judge Jones has been involved in children's issues for 4 years, 3 of those as the Presiding Judge at Juvenile Court. He is involved in numerous social and civic organizations. He has also served as statewide secretary of the Juvenile Court Judges of California, and has been a frequent instructor in juvenile law for the California Center for Judicial Education and Research, which trains other judges for the important and challenging work of the Juvenile Court.

12 corn tortillas
1/2 cup Wesson oil
2 cups (8-ounce) shredded Kraft
    Monterey Jack cheese
1/2 cup Crystal butter
3/4 cup chopped onion
1/2 cup flour
2 cups dairy Crystal sour cream
4 cups chicken broth
1 (4-ounce) can jalapeno peppers
    (optional)
1 pound hamburger
3 bunches green onions
1 small can sliced olives

In skillet cook tortillas one at a time in hot oil for 15 seconds on each side (do not overcook or they won't roll).

Place 2 tablespoons shredded cheese and 1 tablespoon chopped onion and large spoonful of hamburger (It's good to fry onion and hamburger together) and a few olives on each tortilla, roll up.

Place seam side down in baking dish. In sauce pan melt butter, blend in flour. Add chicken broth.

Cook, stirring constantly until mixture thickens and bubbles appear. Stir in sour cream and peppers. Cook until heated thoroughly, but DO NOT BOIL.

Pour over tortillas in baking dish. Bake in 425° oven for 20 minutes.

Sprinkle remaining cheese on top with green onions, return to oven for 5 minutes or until cheese melts. The sauce should cover the tortillas completely.

Holiday Recipes

Italian Spinach Stuffing

Stacey Lynn

My career in radio began four years ago in San Luis Obispo where I grew up. Working at 97.7 KWIN as both the Promotions Director and Midday DJ, keeps me extremely busy. So I don't get many nights at home in the kitchen to cook.

3 bunches spinach
1 small bunch of celery
2 medium white onions
1/2 bunch of parsley
1 box of seasoned stuffing bread
1/2 cup chopped walnuts
3 IGA California eggs
Italian seasonings
Salt and pepper

Steam spinach and drain well, Pan fry cut up vegetables; celery, onions, parsley, then combine all the ingredients including eggs, bread, walnuts and seasonings. Mix well. Stuff turkey and cook away!! (Extra stuffing can be cooked separately in a casserole.)

Holiday Spinach Salad

Jean Runyon

Jean Runyon has been a much-acclaimed advertising/public relations professional since she began her career in the mid-1950s. Her many years of public service and her outstanding efforts in business communications have won her the respect and admiration of business leaders, local officials and clients alike. This is a very festive salad for the holidays . It is colorful, flavorful, and easy to do.

1/4 cup champagne vinegar
4 teaspoons IGA sugar
1 teaspoon dry Schilling mustard
salt & white pepper to taste
2 teaspoons lemon juice
2/3 cup Wesson oil

Salad:
1 pound fresh spinach, stems removed and torn into bite-sized pieces
1 cup red seedless grapes
1/4 pound bacon, cooked crisp and crumbled
1 large avocado, sliced
1/4 red onion, sliced into thin rings
fresh grated Kraft Romano cheese or Kraft Parmesan cheese

For dressing combine vinegar, sugar, mustard, salt & pepper in blender. Add lemon juice. With machine running, gradually add oil.

For salad combine all salad ingredients except cheese. Pour dressing over salad and toss gently. Grate or shave cheese with vegetable peeler over each serving. ENJOY!!

Fresh Cranberry Sauce

1 package fresh cranberries, rinse and check for stems and bad berries
1 cup IGA sugar
1/2 cup water
2 teaspoons lemon juice
1/8 teaspoon salt

Yvonne Sinclair
Rocklin, CA

Place in sauce pan, mix well, and bring to a boil. Boil until the berries are popping and remove from heat. Cool and refrigerate until needed. Makes about 2 cups of sauce.

Holiday Punch

Attorney General Dan Lungren

On January 7, 1991, Dan Lungren became California's 29th Attorney General. Prior to that Lungren was a partner in the Sacramento law firm of Diepenbrock, Wulff, Plant and Hannegan.

1 can orange juice
2 quarts cranberry juice
1/3 cup lemon juice
1 cup water
3 whole nutmegs
2 whole cloves
1 1/2 sticks cinnamon

Pre-wrap cloves, nutmegs, and cinnamon sticks in cheesecloth and place in 30 cup percolator. Combine all ingredients and heat. Make a festive, nonalcoholic, warm holiday drink. Serves: 30

Egg Nog Chocolate Chip Cookies

Anita Barnes

Executive Director, La Familia counseling Center, Inc., Barnes is active, working in the community for over 20 years on behalf of at risk youth and families.

2 1/2 cups all purpose flour
1 teaspoon baking soda
1 cup softened Crystal butter
3/4 cup IGA sugar
3/4 cup firmly packed IGA brown sugar
1 1/2 tablespoons egg nog
1 IGA California egg
2 cups chocolate chips
1 1/2 cups pecans
1 1/2 cups coconut flakes

Preheat oven to 375° Combine flour, baking soda and salt set aside. In large bowl mix, butter, brown sugar and egg nog until creamy. Beat in egg. Slowly add flour mixture. Stir in chocolate chips, nuts and coconut. Drop by rounded tablespoons onto ungreased cookie sheet. Bake about 10 minutes. Makes: 4 dozen

Holiday Wreath Cake

2 extra large bananas, peeled
4 large IGA California eggs
1 1/2 cups IGA sugar
1 cup Wesson oil
1/4 cup pineapple juice
1 teaspoon rum extract
3 cups flour
1 1/2 teaspoons baking soda
1/2 teaspoons baking powder
1 1/2 teaspoons ground Schilling
    cinnamon
1/2 teaspoons salt
1 package, 8-ounce, chopped
    dates
1 1/2 cups chopped almonds
1 cup raisins

Sugar Plum Glaze:
1/2 cup prunes
1/4 cup pineapple juice
1 cup powdered IGA sugar

Genevieve Greenlee
Sacramento, CA

Puree bananas in blender (1 1/4 cups). In large mixing bowl, beat eggs until creamy yellow. Beat in sugar and oil. Beat in bananas, pineapple juice and rum extract.

Combine dry ingredients. Beat into banana mixture. Stir in dates, chopped almonds, and raisins. Turn batter into greased 10-inch bundt pan.

Bake in 325° for 65-75 minutes or until pick comes out clean. Cool 20 minutes then turn out onto a wire rack.

Cool completely. Spread with glaze. Garnish top of cake with sliced almonds.

For sugar plum glaze, process all ingredients in food processor until smooth.

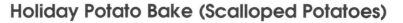

Holiday Potato Bake (Scalloped Potatoes)

1 cup chopped onion
1/4 cup Crystal butter
1 can cream of celery soup
4 pounds Idaho potatoes, cooked,
    peeled, chopped
1 1/2 cups shredded Kraft cheddar
    cheese
1/2 cup crushed corn flakes
3 tablespoons melted Crystal butter

Cook onions in 1/4 cup butter, remove from stove. Add sour cream, soup. Mix well. Combine potato soup, mix well. Put into greased 9x13-inch baking dish. Chill overnight. Top with crumbs. Lightly pour melted butter over top. Bake 350° for 1 hour.

Dicky Krenz
Linden, CA

Super Bowl Chili

Maureen Reagan

I always cook chili for the Super Bowl. This recipe was even cooked by me in 1987 in the main kitchen of the White House.

3 pounds lean hamburger
1 pound each pinto beans, kidney beans, small red
    beans
2 pounds pear tomatoes
3 (16-ounce) cans tomato puree
1 cup salsa
6 cloves garlic, minced
3 large onions, chopped
2 large bell peppers, chopped
2 teaspoons Schilling oregano, or to taste
2 teaspoons Schilling chili powder, or to taste
salt and pepper to taste

Brown hamburger, add garlic and spices. In large pot mix raw vegetables, beans. Add meat mixture, tomato sauce and salsa. Add 2 cups water. Cook at 250° to 275° for 3 hours, stir occasionally. Serve with rice or bread. As a side dish with hamburgers or chicken. Serves: 16

Apple Cake

2 cups IGA sugar
1/2 cup Wesson oil
2 IGA California eggs
4 cups diced apples
2 cups flour
1 teaspoon salt
2 teaspoons Schilling cinnamon
1 teaspoon nutmeg
2 teaspoons baking soda

Shelley Spindler
Meadow Vista, CA

Combine sugar, oil and eggs. Add apples. Sift together flour, salt, cinnamon, nutmeg and baking soda.

Add sifted dry ingredients to apple mixture. Put into 9 x 13 greased cake pan and bake for 1 hour in a pre-heated 350° oven.

Bright Jewel Cookies

2 cups flour
1/2 teaspoon baking powder
1/2 teaspoon salt
1 cup Crystal butter (softened)
2 tablespoons orange juice
grated peel of one orange
grated peel of one lemon
1/2 cup IGA sugar
1 teaspoon vanilla
2 IGA California egg yolks
1 IGA California egg white slightly
    beaten
1 1/4 cups nuts (chopped fine)
candied cherries (red and green)

Carol Dominick
Stockton, CA

Combine flour, baking powder and salt. Cream together butter, sugar, orange juice, grated peel, vanilla and egg yolks. Add flour mix.

Chill dough thoroughly.

Form dough into small balls, roll in egg white and then in chopped nuts. Place on cookie sheet press piece of candied cherry in center and depress slightly.

Bake in oven at 350° for 10-12 minutes.

Desserts

Bopcorn (Bertice's Popcorn)

Dr. Bertice Berry

"Bopcorn is a combination of a recipe I found and things I've added over the years. I'm allergic to chocolate, but I enjoy watching others eat it! Then I can let them eat for me — enjoy!"

1 bowl of freshly popped popcorn
1 bag miniature pretzels
1 can mixed nuts
2 sticks Kraft margarine
2 cups brown IGA sugar
1 teaspoon baking soda
1/2 bag M&Ms (with or without nuts)
any other chocolate you're not allergic to

Mix popcorn, pretzels and nuts in large bowl.

Melt margarine and add in baking soda, stir another 2 minutes. Add this mixture to dry mixture.

Stir so that caramel mixture covers popcorn completely. Add in chocolates and stir until melted.

Place mixture on waxed paper-lined cookie sheet. Let cool (refrigerate until ready if you can't wait). Pass it out until you all pass out.

Dann's Wife's Sky High Heavenly Mint Brownies

Dann Shively

Pilot and reporter Dann Shively has been a part of Sacramento radio and television for over 22 years. He recently joined News Ten and shares his aerial views of Northern California nightly.

1 brownie mix
1/2 teaspoon peppermint extract
1 cup chopped nuts (optional)

Filling:
4 tablespoons Crystal butter
2 cups IGA powdered sugar
2 tablespoons Crystal cream or
    Crystal milk
1 1/2 teaspoons extract of peppermint
green food coloring

Chocolate Topping:
3 squares unsweetened chocolate
2 tablespoons Crystal butter

Bake brownie mix in 9x13-inch pan and cool. Mix filling ingredients together and spread on cooled brownies.

Melt chocolate and butter in double boiler, spread over well chilled brownies.

Cut at room temperature, with hot knife, to stop chocolate from cracking. (To heat knife, dip into boiling water and dry.)

Serves: depends on how big you cut them.

Tri-Berry Pie

Crust:
2 cups flour
1/4 teaspoon salt
1/3 cup & 1 tablespoon shortening
1/3 cup & 1 tablespoon Crystal butter 1/4 cup water

Filling:
2 1/2 cups fruit (strawberries, blackberries, peaches-
amounts as desired to equal 2 1/2 cups)
1 cup IGA sugar
1/2 teaspoon Schilling cinnamon
1/2 cube Crystal butter
2 tablespoons flour

Crust: Mix dry ingredients, fold in shortening and butter, add water slowly to doughy consistency. Makes bottom and top crust.

Filling: Slice fruit, add sugar and cinnamon, pour into pie pan with bottom crust. Sprinkle flour and slices of butter over filling. Cover with top crust, poke holes or make slices in crust.

Bake at 450° for 10 minutes, lower temperature to 350° and bake for 1/2 hour to 45 minutes or until fruit is soft. Enjoy! Serves: 12

Robin Matthews

Robin Matthews hosts the food segment of a half-hour public affairs shows which airs on Channel 10 called "Basic Colors".

Beth's Favorite Chocolate Cookies

Beth Ruyak

1 IGA California egg
1 cup IGA brown sugar
1/2 cup melted Crystal butter
1 1/2 cups flour
1/2 cup Crystal milk
1/2 cup cocoa
1/2 teaspoon baking soda
1 teaspoon baking powder
1 teaspoon vanilla

Icing:
1 tablespoon soft Crystal butter
3 tablespoons lowfat Crystal milk
1 1/2 cups IGA powdered sugar
few drops of food coloring

Combine egg, brown sugar and butter. Add flour, milk, cocoa, baking soda, baking powder and vanilla. Mix ingredients and then drop by teaspoon onto foiled tray. Bake at 350° for 10 minutes. Frost. Store cookies in refrigerator for freshness.

Mango Pie

2 1/2 cups sliced thin, ripe, fresh
   mango
1 tablespoon lemon juice
1/4 cup IGA sugar
3 tablespoons cornstarch
2 teaspoons Crystal butter
1/4 teaspoon almond extract
dash of salt
9-inch pie plate

Crust:
1 1/4 cups all-purpose flour
1/4 teaspoon salt
1/2 teaspoon sugar
3 tablespoons shortening
3 tablespoons Kraft margarine
4 to 5 tablespoons cold water

Cristina Gutierrez
Sacramento, CA

In medium mixing bowl stir together flour, salt and sugar. Cut in shortening, margarine until pieces are the size of small peas. Sprinkle 1 tablespoon of the water over part of the mixture gently toss with a fork. Push to side of bowl. Repeat until all is moistened. Form dough into a ball.

On lightly floured surface flatten dough with hands. Roll dough from edge to edge, forming a circle about 12 inches in diameter. Ease pastry into pie plate, being careful to avoid stretching pastry. Trim pastry even with rim of pie plate. Prick bottom and sides with tins of a fork. Bake at 450° for 10 to 12 minutes.

In mixing bowl combine mango and sugar. Sprinkle mango with lemon juice, toss gently to coat. Let the mango stand about 1 hour. Drain mango, reserving syrup. Add enough water to the reserved syrup to measure 1 cup liquid. Add to cornstarch and blend and cook over low heat until thick stirring constantly. Remove from heat add butter, salt, almond extract. Cool the sauce. Turn mango mixture into baked crust. Pour over cooled mixture. Chill overnight.

Whip 1 cup whipping cream with 1 tablespoon powder sugar. Spread over pie. Top with 8 maraschino cherries.

Kamalo Ranch Cake

Robin Bolton

Robin Bolton of River City Brewing Co. and Chantrelle arrived in Sacramento via New Orleans from Molokai, Hawaii. With a varied background including the cruise line industry, beverage management and ranching, she decided on a career change and attended Lederwalff Culinary Academy and served an apprenticeship there. Robin credits her love of cooking to her mother who raised the family on home grown foods and fresh baked goods. This is a traditional family recipe adapted to the fruits and nuts grown on her ranch on Molokai.

1 cup shortening
1 cup IGA sugar
2 IGA California eggs
1 cup dried pineapple cut up
1 cup hot water
1 teaspoon baking soda
1 3/4 cups plus 2 tablespoons flour
1/2 teaspoon salt
1/2 teaspoon vanilla
1 cup white chocolate chips
1/2 cup chopped macadamia nuts
1/4 cup unsweetened coconut

Pour hot water and soda over pineapple and let sit until cool. Cream shortening and sugar, add eggs and vanilla. Stir in dry ingredients alternately with pineapple mixture. Pour into lightly greased 9x13-inch pan, sprinkle with chips, nuts and coconut. Bake at 350° for 40 minutes.

153

Boiled Spice Cake

2 cups water
1 cup IGA sugar
1 cup shortening
1 cup raisins (optional)
4 tablespoons spices (all the same spice or any combination of Schilling cinnamon, Schilling allspice, cloves or pumpkin)

Jan Scott
Grass Valley, CA

Combine ingredients and bring to a boil until sugar is dissolved. Let cool 15 minutes. When cooled add: 3 cups flour and 1 teaspoon baking soda.

Variations, Add: 1 cup chopped apples, chopped dates, chopped nuts, chopped candied fruit (Christmas Fruit cake) or anything you'd like.

When adding dates and nuts, pour rum over cooled cake and let it set in refrigerator for a couple of days. Delicious date, nut rum cake.

Oatmeal Pie

Larry and Katie Kelly

This recipe was developed by Laura Fitch over 40 years ago and has also been in "Gourmet" magazine. We have been chef's/owners at Monte Vista for 22 years.

4 IGA California eggs
1 cube Crystal butter, melted
1/2 cup IGA sugar
1 cup quick oats
1 1/2 cups syrup
1 teaspoon Schilling cinnamon
1/2 teaspoon ground cloves

Whisk all ingredients together and pour into unbaked 9-inch pie shell. Bake at 350° for 1 hour. Serves: 6-7

Chocolate Fondue Chocolate

Friar Tucks Restaurant and Bar

For 20 years, Friar Tuck's has served fondue and chocolate is a favorite. The recipe is actually from Belgium even though fondue is typically Swiss.

2 cups semisweet or bittersweet (or mixture of the two)
1 cup Crystal heavy cream
3 tablespoons liquor of choice (Whisky, Brandy, Amaretto, etc...)
Pound cake, cubed
Assorted fresh fruits, cut up
Chopped nuts

Melt chocolate and cream together in double boiler. Add liquor just before serving. Arrange cake and fruit on plate. Dip fruits in chocolate, then nuts. Everybody has fun dipping. Serves: 2-4

Mom's Charlotte Russe

Gregory Favre

What is a newspaper editor doing cooking desserts? Well, when you are born in New Orleans and grow up in a house with nine brothers and sisters and a mother who was absolutely one of the great cake makers of all time, it just comes naturally. And it helps if you love sweets, as I do.

3 1/2 pints Crystal whipping cream
14 IGA California egg yolks
6 IGA California egg whites
1 tablespoon IGA sugar for every yolk
vanilla, to taste
1 cup Crystal milk for every two IGA California eggs
3 envelopes of gelatin soaked in 1/2 cup cold water

Scald milk, add to sugar and eggs mixture; add vanilla; put gelatin into hot mixture.

Refrigerate until it congeals, but not hard; beat egg white and fold into mixture; whip 3 1/2 pints whipping cream and fold in.

Mix well and put into large bowl lined with lady fingers, or use a 10-inch spring-form pan.

Refrigerate until congealed and ready to serve.

Not Just Brownies

Brownies:
1 cup Crystal butter
4 IGA California eggs
2 cups IGA sugar
8 heaping tablespoons cocoa
1 teaspoon salt
2 cups flour
2 teaspoon vanilla
1 cup walnuts (optional)

Frosting:
1/4 cup Crystal butter
2 envelopes (1-ounce each) Nestles Choco Bake (or 2 ounces baking chocolate)
3 cups sifted IGA powdered sugar
1/3 cup Crystal milk
1 teaspoon vanilla

Joanne Waters
Stockton CA

Melt and cool butter. Beat eggs. Add sugar, cocoa and salt. Add melted butter, flour, vanilla and walnuts.

Bake in 350° oven, 15 - 20 minutes.

Do NOT OVERBAKE, let cool.

Not Just Brownies Frosting: Melt butter in 2 quart saucepan and remove from heat. Add chocolate and stir until blended.

Alternately add powdered sugar and milk. Stir in vanilla.

Refrigerate & eat. These are not just brownies.! They're more like fudge!

Tropical Fruit Sushi With Ginger And "Wasabi"

Patricia Diane Murakami

Chinois East/West

Pastry Chef Patricia Diane Murakami began working in the restaurant business in her family's Northern Italian restaurant in New Jersey. After relocating to California, she worked as a cook at the Domaine Chandon sparkling winery in the Napa Valley, where she soon crossed over into pastries. In her current job as pastry chef for Chinois East/West, Chef Murakami experiments with the incorporation of unique Asian ingredients into her desserts. Asian foods have had a revitalizing effect on California cuisine, bringing a new aesthetic and a wealth of flavors, helping to give rise to the Pacific Rim culinary movement.

7 ounces bittersweet chocolate
5 tablespoons light corn syrup
1 13.5 ounces can of Chaokoh brand coconut milk
13.5 ounces of Crystal heavy cream (measure cream into coconut milk can)
6 tablespoons IGA sugar
1/2 cup Jasmine rice
1 1/2 kiwi, sliced in 1/4 inch strips
1 mango, sliced in 1/4 inch strips
6 strawberries, sliced in 1/4 inch strips
1/4 cup simple syrup (equal parts of water and IGA sugar, mixed until sugar is dissolved)
1/4 cup dark rum
1/2 kiwi
3 tablespoons candied ginger, diced

Melt the chocolate in a stainless steel bowl over simmering water. While the chocolate is still warm, stir in the corn syrup. The mixture will thicken.

Divide in half, wrap each part in plastic wrap and set aside at room temperature for 2 or 3 hours before assembling.

The chocolate mixture will become very hard after cooling but will soften up by kneading it for a few minutes just before you roll it out.

(Note: This will keep at room temperature for several days.)

Combine the coconut milk, cream, sugar, and rice in a medium saucepan and place over medium heat. Simmer for about 30 minutes stirring frequently as the rice has a tendency to stick to the bottom of the pan.

The rice pudding will become very thick with full, soft rice kernels.

Pour into a container and cover with plastic wrap directly on the rice pudding to prevent a skin from forming. Refrigerate until cool, approximately two hours.

About 1/2 to 1 hour before assembling sushi, marinate the julienned fruit in dark rum and simple syrup. (The fruits listed here are just a suggestion; any of your favorite fruits will do well here.) Shortly before assembly, strain the fruit. Puree the remaining 1/2 kiwi, and reserve.

Assembly: Dust the counter and rolling pin with powdered sugar just as though you were rolling out dough. Roll out the chocolate to a little larger than 6" X 10" and trim to 6" X 10 ".

Spread 1 cup of the rice pudding over the chocolate leaving about 1/4" along one of the 10" sides empty. Place the fruit down the center lengthwise and roll up jelly roll style.

Trim 1/8" from both ends of the sushi and brush any remaining powdered sugar from the chocolate with a pastry brush or soft towel. Repeat with the second half of the chocolate.

Slice in one inch pieces. To serve, place 3 pieces of sushi on each plate, garnished with a little diced candied ginger and a little of the reserved kiwi puree ("wasabi"). Serves: 6

Flapper Pie

12 large graham crackers
1/2 cup IGA sugar
1/4 cup melted Crystal butter
3 tablespoons cornstarch
3/4 cup IGA brown sugar
1 tablespoon melted Crystal butter
2 cups Crystal milk
2 IGA California egg yolks
1 teaspoon vanilla
2 IGA California egg whites
4 tablespoons IGA sugar

Esther Dowden
Sacramento, CA

Roll graham crackers until fine, add sugar and melted butter, mix well. Place 1/2 the mixture in pie pan molding to pan as if pastry.

Place cornstarch, brown sugar, milk, egg yolks and 1 tablespoon melted butter in double boiler.

Cook until thick, add vanilla. Fill the lined pie pan with mixture.

Beat egg whites until stiff, add sugar and place on top of custard mixture.

Sprinkle butter with remaining half of graham cracker mixture. Bake in 300° oven until browned.

Serve cold. Serves: 8

Mississippi Mud Pie

2 cups vanilla wafer crumbs (38)
4 tablespoons Crystal butter
1 quart fresh strawberries
1 (8-ounce) Kraft cream cheese (light) softened
1 (14-ounce) can condensed milk
1/2 cup fresh lime juice
1 tablespoon green creme de menthe
1 cup Crystal whipping cream
3 tablespoons IGA granulated sugar
1/2 teaspoon vanilla
Fresh mint

Bev Williams
Penn Valley, CA

Crust: Combine crumbs, butter, press into pie plate.

Rinse and dry strawberries, arrange on bottom. Save 2 or 3 for garnish. Beat cream cheese until smooth. Add condensed milk, lime and mint liqueur, blend. Top with whipped cream and sugar or cool whip. Garnish with strawberries.

Orange-Walnut Pudding Cake

1/2 cup (1 cube) Crystal butter or
    Kraft margarine
1 1/4 cups IGA sugar
2 IGA California eggs
1 tablespoon grated orange peel
2 1/2 cups cake flour
2 tablespoons baking powder
1 teaspoon baking soda
1/2 teaspoon salt
1 cup orange juice
1 cup chopped walnut meats

Orange syrup:
1 cup IGA sugar
2 cup water
1 teaspoon grated orange peel

Mary McGuffin
Sierra City, CA

Cream butter and sugar together until light and fluffy. Beat in eggs, one at a time. Add grated orange peel and beat thoroughly. Sift cake flour, measure and sift again with baking powder, soda and salt. Add dry ingredients to creamed mixture alternately with orange juice, stir in walnut meats. Turn into a buttered 9-inch square baking pan. Bake in a moderate oven 350° for 45 minutes, or until a toothpick inserted in the center comes out clean. Allow cake to cool slightly, and spoon orange syrup over top. Cut cake in squares to serve. Serves: 8

To make orange syrup, combine sugar, water and orange peel and boil 15 minutes. Spoon over slightly cooled cake.

Mud Cake

Granny Garbage

Granny Garbage is the recycling Queen of San Joaquin.

Cake:
2 cubes butter (1 c.)
2 tablespoons cocoa
2 cups sugar
4 eggs
1 teaspoon vanilla
1 1/2 cups flour
1 1/3 cups coconut
1 1/2 cups chopped walnuts

Filling:
1 large jar marshmallow creme

Frosting:
1 box powdered sugar
1/2 cup butter
1 teaspoon vanilla
1/2 cup evaporated milk
1/3 cup cocoa

Cream butter and sugar for cake. Add cocoa. Add eggs and vanilla; mix well. Add flour, coconut, and nuts. Bake in a 9x13-inch greased and floured pan at 350° (325° in glass dish) for 30-40 minutes. When done, immediately spread with marshmallow creme. Let cool. Frost with frosting ingredients mixed together. Dirt never tasted so GOOD!

Easy "Good For You" Cookies

4 cups oatmeal, quick
2 cups IGA brown sugar, packed
    down
1 cup Wesson safflower oil
1 cup coconut
1 cup chopped walnuts
1 teaspoon vanilla
1/2 teaspoon salt (optional)
2 extra large IGA California eggs or 3
    small IGA California eggs

Jane May (Mrs. J.R. May)
Stockton, CA

In large bowl: mix oatmeal, brown sugar, and oil. Cover with plastic wrap 8 hours or overnight.

Next day: Add coconut, walnuts, vanilla, and eggs.

Stir with spoon (no mixer).

Drop by teaspoons on greased cookie sheet (sprayed with Pam).

Bake at 350° for about 13 minutes varies by size of cookie you want.

Let cool slightly before removing. Freezes well. Great with ice cream! Serves: 144

Judy's Famous Pearcake

2 cups mashed fresh or canned
    Bartlett pears
1 cup shortening
1 1/2 cups IGA sugar
2 IGA California eggs
2 cups flour
2 teaspoons Schilling cinnamon
2 teaspoons baking soda
1 teaspoon salt

Topping:
1/2 cup IGA brown sugar
1 cup chopped walnuts

Judy Culbertson
Courtland, CA

Preheat oven to 350°.

Cream shortening and sugar. Add eggs. Beat until fluffy.

Add dry ingredients; mix well. Add pear pulp.

Blend well (you'll need to use your muscles!). Pour into greased 9 x 13 inch

Sprinkle topping over unbaked cake and bake for 35-40 minutes.

Canned pears contain no preservatives and are an ideal substitute for fresh Bartlett pears.

Mom's Divinity Fudge

Suzanne Adan

In 1958, as a 2nd year member of 4-H, I enrolled in a food preparation class and learned to cook. 36 years later and a few extra added pounds, I still cook and bake for my husband, Artist Michael Stevens. I've been an artist for 24 years and am represented by the Michael Himovitz Gallery. My mother has been making this candy at Christmas for as long as I can remember. She got the recipe from her Home Economics teacher, Mrs. Audrey Harper, at Mohawk High School in Marcola, Oregon.

2 cups IGA sugar
1/2 cup corn syrup
1/2 cup water
2 IGA California egg whites, stiffly
   beaten
1 teaspoon vanilla
1/2 cup chopped walnuts
1/8 teaspoon salt

Boil sugar, water and syrup to 250° or to the hard ball stage. This ball will make a crackling sound when tapped against the side of a cup.

Pour syrup slowly over beaten egg whites, beating constantly. When mixture begins to lose its gloss, fold in vanilla, nuts and salt.

Drop by teaspoonfuls onto waxed paper or turn into lightly buttered pan.

*Note: Brown sugar may be substituted for half the white sugar. Dates, figs or other fruits may be added.

One square of chocolate melted, to which 1/4 teaspoon of butter has been added, can be spread over divinity.

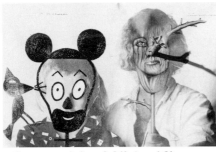
Suzanne Adan & Michael Stevens

Yuless of Loggus

Michael Stevens

I've been an artist and teacher for 25 years. I'm married to artist Suzanne Adan and we have 2 spunky wirehaired fox terriers — Reilly and Murphy. The only thing I do in the kitchen is make toast or fix eggs. In 1990, a friend had an All-Dessert Holiday Party and I devised this recipe to take. It was such a hit that friends have been begging me to create this holiday treat ever since.

8 Twinkies
4 small chocolate pudding cups
1 can chocolate frosting spread
1 milk carton of chocolate malted milk balls

Place 4 of the twinkies on a plate.

Spread pudding on top.

Place the rest of the twinkies on top of the layer of pudding.

Spread the top, sides and ends with frosting.

Apply malted milk balls generously to the entire log.

Refrigerate for several hours. Slice and serve.

Italian Cream Cake

Kitty O'Neal

Currently the afternoon News host on KFBK A.M. 1530, where I've worked since 1984. I also do freelance TV and radio work. My mom made this cake for my birthday years ago and it's been a favorite since!

1 stick Kraft margarine
1/2 cup Shortening
2 cups IGA sugar
5 IGA California eggs, separated
1 cup buttermilk
1 teaspoon baking soda
2 cups flour
1 teaspoon vanilla
1 small can angel flake coconut or 1 c.
1 cup chopped pecans

Frosting:
8 ounces Kraft cream cheese
1 pound IGA powdered sugar
6 tablespoons Kraft margarine
1 teaspoon vanilla

Cream margarine, Crisco and sugar. Gradually add egg yolks and beat well. Add soda to buttermilk, then add flour and milk alternately. Add vanilla.

Add pecans and coconut. Fold in well beaten egg whites.
Makes 3 layers or on 13x9x2-inch. Bake layers 325° about 25-30 minutes. Bake sheet for about 45 minutes.

For frosting soften cream cheese and margarine. Cream, then beat all and spread on cake. Refrigerate in hot weather. This cake freezes very well.

Butterfinger Candy Balls

1 stick Kraft margarine or Crystal butter
2 cups chunky peanut butter
2 cups IGA powdered sugar
2 1/2 cups crisp rice cereal
1/2 cup crushed nuts
1/2 stick parowax
1 12-ounce package chocolate chips

Peggy Smith

Mix everything except the parowax and chocolate by hand, form into bite-sized balls.

Place on waxed paper-covered cookie sheet. Chill in freezer for several hours or overnight.

When ready to coat in chocolate, melt the wax in the top of a double boiler and then add chocolate chips, melt. Continue to heat chocolate mixture over low heat while dipping balls.

Dip chilled balls into chocolate mixture with fork, twirl to coat. Place again on waxed paper-coated cookie sheet. Place in freezer.

When frozen, store in plastic bag. Thaw before eating.

Aunt Bill's Brown Candy

6 cups IGA granulated sugar
2 cups Crystal cream or evaporated
  milk
1 tablespoon white corn syrup
1/2 cup (1 stick) Crystal butter or
  Kraft margarine
1/4 teaspoon baking soda
1 teaspoon vanilla
2 cups broken pecans

Dr. G. Henry Wells
Fair Oaks, CA

Put 2 cups of the sugar in a heavy pan. A good heavy iron skillet is good to use. Set it over low heat and let it melt gradually. Do not stir sugar until it begins to turn to liquid. Then stir with a wooden spoon until it caramelizes. Expect this to take about 30 minutes.

This is the flavor secret of this candy. While the sugar caramelizes, place the remaining 4 cups sugar, cream or evaporated milk, and corn syrup in another larger sauce pan or kettle and bring to a boil. When the sugar is all caramelized it is ready to add to the boiling syrup. Pour the caramelized sugar in a very thin stream into the boiling syrup (do not let it get too thick), stirring constantly.

It is easier if two people make this candy during these first two steps. After the two sugar syrups are mixed, continue cooking over medium heat to 242° on a candy thermometer or until a firm ball is formed when a little is dropped into cold water. Remove from heat and add butter (cut into pieces to melt easier) and soda. Stir only until butter melts. Cool undisturbed 20 minutes. Add vanilla and nuts and beat until thick and creamy. Pour into greased pans to become firm. Makes 4 pounds

Joe's Favorite Coffee Cake

Joe and Helen Crane

Joe is President of Union Safe Deposit Bank. Helen is a member of the San Joaquin County CAPC Board of Directors.

2 1/2 cups flour
1 cup IGA brown sugar
3/4 cup IGA white sugar
1 cup Wesson oil
1 cup buttermilk
1 teaspoon baking powder
1 teaspoon baking soda
1 IGA California egg
1 teaspoon salt
1/2 teaspoon Schilling nutmeg

Topping:
1/2 cup walnuts
2 tablespoons flour
2 teaspoons Schilling cinnamon

Mix together flour, brown sugar, white sugar and oil until all oil has been absorbed. Then, take out one full cup of the mixture and set aside for the topping. Add buttermilk, baking powder, baking soda, egg, salt and nutmeg to the mixture. Mix together and put in baking dish. Mix walnuts, flour, cinnamon and the cup of cake mixture that was set aside for the topping to be put on the cake before you put it in the oven:

Bake in large pyrex dish approximately 9 1/2x15-inch at 350° for 25-30 minutes, or when lightly pressed, the cake feels firm. Serves: 12-14

Banana Split Cake

Crust:
1 cup flour
1 cube Kraft margarine
1/2 cup chopped nuts

Filling:
2 cups bananas
2 cubes Kraft margarine
2 IGA California eggs

Bessie Casey
Ceres, CA

Mix together crust ingredients, press into 9x13-inch pan. Bake until light brown, cool.

Beat filling ingredients at high speed 15 minutes. Spread evenly over cooled crust. Let cool in refrigerator until cooled and set. Cover with sliced bananas then cover with crushed drained pineapples. About 20 ounces Top with 8 ounces cool whip, 1/2 cup chopped nuts, and maraschino cherries.

Baked Alaska

Miles Smith

Miles love of fresh fruits and vegetables carries over to cooking. He started work at the restaurant "Charles at the Crossroads" and that is where he learned to make his Baked Alaska. It is always a show stopper. Smith is president of Cal Fresh Produce, northern California's finest wholesale purveyor of produce.

Sponge Cake:
1 cup cake flour
1/4 teaspoons salt
6 IGA California eggs, separated
1 cup IGA superfine sugar
1 tablespoon lemon juice
IGA confectioners' sugar

Meringue Topping:
3 IGA California egg whites
1/2 cup IGA superfine sugar

Filling:
2 tablespoons dark rum (optional)
1 quart Crystal ice cream (raspberry ripple, chocolate or fruit)

To make cake: grease and lightly flour bottom of 9 x 12-inch cake pan. Sift flour and salt together. Beat egg yolks until thick and lemon-colored.

Beat egg whites in large mixing bowl with electric mixer at high speed until stiff but not dry. Add superfine sugar, about 2 tablespoons at a time; beat thoroughly after each addition. Beat in lemon juice and rind. Fold in egg yolks with rubber spatula or wire whisk. Cut and fold in flour mixture, small amount at a time. Continue folding 2 minutes after last addition.

Fill prepared pan 3/4 full; smooth batter evenly into corners and over top. (There will be batter left over.) Bake in preheated 350° oven 30 - 35 minutes or until cake test done.

To prepare the meringue topping, beat the egg whites until stiff peaks form. Add the sugar a tablespoon at a time, beating well after each addition. Beat until the sugar is dissolved and the meringue is stiff and glossy.

Filling: Place the sponge cake layer on a baking sheet. Sprinkle the rum over the cake, if used. Using firm ice cream, pile on top of the cake to within 1/2 inch of the edge. Spread the meringue over the top and sides of the ice cream and cake, covering them completely; leave no holes.

Bake in a 500° oven for 3-5 minutes, until the meringue is delicately browned. Serve immediately. This dessert is very impressive, even though it is easy to make. Serves: 8

Banana Cake

Kathleen Brown

Kathleen Brown is the State Treasurer of California. This recipe is actually from her mother, Bernice Brown, during her days as First Lady of California. The Brown family uses this recipe for all birthdays.

1/2 cup Crystal butter
1 1/2 cups IGA sugar
2 IGA California eggs, separate and beat whites
1/2 cup sour Crystal milk or 1/2 cup buttermilk
1 teaspoon baking soda
2 cups flour
2 teaspoons Calumet baking powder
3 mashed bananas
1 teaspoon vanilla
1 cup chopped walnuts

Icing:
2 tablespoons Crystal butter
2 1/2 cups confectioner's IGA sugar
1 whole IGA California egg
1 teaspoon vanilla
Crystal cream or top milk

Cream butter and sugar. Add egg yolks, then milk with baking soda. Mix. Add flour and baking powder sifted together. Add vanilla, bananas and nuts and beat well. Fold in beaten egg whites. Bake in 3 greased layer pans in a 325° to 350° oven until done, about 30 minutes.

To make icing cream butter and sugar. Add whole egg. Mix. Add vanilla. Add cream until icing is the right consistency to spread.

Teddy's Almost Famous — Almost Fat Free Chocolate Chip Cheesecake Cupcakes

1 chocolate cake mix, or your favorite chocolate cake recipe
1 (12-ounce) package semisweet chocolate chips
1 (8-ounce) package fat-free Kraft cream cheese
1/2 cup IGA sugar
2 tablespoons fat-free mayonnaise
1/2 cup Crystal milk
1 IGA California egg
1 package of cupcake baking cups

Teddy Johnston
Sacramento, CA

Mix cake according to directions (delete cooking oil) in place of oil add 2 tablespoons fat-free mayonnaise and 1/2 cup of milk. Beat on high for 3 minutes.

In separate mixing bowl beat egg, sugar, and cream cheese (at room temperature) until fluffy. Fold most of chocolate chips into mixture (eating a handful or two as you go along!).

Spoon cupcake cups about half full with chocolate cake mix, then spoon a heaping tablespoon full of chocolate chip cream cheese mixture. Cover with chocolate cake mix to top of cup.

Preheat oven at 350°, bake for 20 minutes. Enjoy! Store in Ziplock baggies to preserve moisture!!!

Deep Dish Peach Cobbler

Kevin M. Johnson

Kevin Johnson was born March 4, 1966 in Sacramento, CA. He graduated Sacramento High School in 1983. He attended the University of California at Berkeley. In February 1988, he was traded from the Cleveland Caveliers basketball team to the Phoenix Suns where he has remained since. In Phoenix, Kevin serves on the Board of Directors of the Phoenix Symphony, the Phoenix Suns Charities and the School House Foundation. He has served as an advisor to the Governor's Youth Commission Against Drugs, instituted KJ's Readers, a reading program in a local school district, and has implemented a book scholarship for junior/senior high school college bound students at a local prep school.

Pastry:
2 cups all-purpose flour
1/2 teaspoons salt
2/3 cup shortening
4-6 tablespoons water

Filling:
2 cans (29 ounces each) peach slices in syrup
1/2 cup firmly packed brown sugar
2 tablespoons all-purpose flour
1/4 teaspoon nutmeg
1 tablespoon butter or margarine

Heat oven to 400°. For pastry, combine flour and salt in medium bowl. Cut in butter until mixture resembles coarse crumbs. Sprinkle with water while mixing lightly with fork. Form into ball. Roll 2/3 of dough into 13-inch square on lightly floured surface. Place in 8-inch square baking dish.

For filling, drain peaches, reserving 1/2 cup syrup. Combine brown sugar, flour, nutmeg, and salt in large bowl. Add peaches. Mix lightly. Spoon into pastry shell. Dot with butter. Roll remaining dough into 9-inch square. Cut into eight strips. Place strips across fruit to form lattice. Seal and flute edges of pastry. Bake at 400° for 40 to 45 minutes or until golden brown.

Grandma's Apple Dumplings

6 medium, tart, juicy apples
1 cup IGA sugar
2 cups water
3 tablespoons Crystal butter
1 3/4 teaspoons Schilling cinnamon
1 tablespoon Crystal butter

Pastry:
2 cups sifted flour
1 teaspoon salt
2/3 cup lard or 2/3 cup plus 2
   tablespoons shortening
1/4 cup water

Sheri Rose
Sacramento, CA

For pastry, measure flour into bowl and mix with salt. Cut in shortening until size of giant peas. Sprinkle with water, 1 tablespoon at a time. Mix lightly with a fork until flour is moistened.

Heat oven to 425°. Roll out pastry a little less than 1/8" thick and cut into 7" squares. Peel and core an apple for each dumpling. Boil sugar, water, butter and cinnamon for 3 minutes. Place an apple on each pastry square. Fill cavities of apples with mixture of sugar and cinnamon. Dot each with butter.

Bring opposite ends of pastry up over the apple. Overlap, moisten and seal. Lift carefully. Place a little apart in a baking dish. Pour hot syrup around dumplings. Bake 40-45 minutes or until the crust is golden brown and apples are cooked through. (Check with a fork.) Serve warm with syrup.

Grandma Blink's Ice Cream

10 IGA California eggs
4 cups IGA sugar
1/2 gallon extra rich Crystal milk
1 quart of Crystal half & half
1 pint Crystal whipping cream
2 tablespoons vanilla
1 tablespoon lemon flavoring

Larcene Dixon
Stockton, CA

Separate eggs. Cream sugar and egg yolks. Beat egg whites and add to yolk mixture. Pour mixture into milk and cook until done. Cook over medium heat stirring continually to keep the mixture from sticking. After the mixture is cooked, let it cool. Pour into electric or manual freezer and freeze. Be sure and use rock salt on the ice.

Strawberry Pizza

Charles Emerson

Superintendent of Schools - Loomis Union School district. Enjoy cooking, gardening and travel. School Administrator for 30 years. Roseville native.

Crust:
1 1/2 cups flour
1 cup Crystal butter or Kraft margarine
1/4 cup brown IGA sugar
1/2 cup chopped pecans

Filling:
1 (8-ounce) package Kraft cream cheese
3/4 cup IGA powdered sugar
1 (8-ounce) container whipped topping

Topping:
1 (3-ounce) package strawberry gelatin
1/2 cup IGA sugar
dash of salt
1 cup water or strawberry juice (divided in half)
4 tablespoons cornstarch
4 cups sliced strawberries (2 baskets)

Crust: Mix all ingredients to form dough. Spread in pizza pan. Bake at 375° for 10 minutes or until golden brown.

Mix cream cheese and powdered sugar; fold in whipping cream. Spread over cooled crust.

Combine gelatin, sugar (if you already sweetened strawberries, don't add the sugar), salt, and 1/2 cup water or strawberry juice.

Dissolve cornstarch in remaining water.

Stir into gelatin mixture; cook over medium heat until thickened.

Stir in strawberries to coat all slices, cool. Spread on top of filling. Chill. Enjoy! Serves: 6-8

Strawberry Cheese Crepes

Crepes:
2 IGA California eggs
1 1/4 cup Crystal milk
1 cup flour
1/2 teaspoon salt
1/4 cup IGA sugar

Filling:
12 ounces Kraft cream cheese
1/4 cup IGA sugar
1 1/2 tablespoons grated lemon rind
3 tablespoons lemon juice

Topping:
1 package frozen strawberries
1/4 teaspoons almond extract
1 tablespoon lemon juice
1/4 cup blanched, sliced almonds

Roma Orvis
Farmington, CA

To make crepes beat eggs and milk. Sift flour, salt and sugar.

Beat into egg mixture until smooth. Make at least one hour ahead or day before. Cover and refrigerate.

Fry in oiled pan or crepe maker. Crepes should be about 6" diameter.

Stack between paper towels.

To make filling beat cream cheese with sugar, lemon rind, and lemon juice.

Fill crepes and roll. Put in flat casserole dish if making ahead. Warm in 500° oven for 10 minutes, covered.

To make topping heat strawberries, almond extract and lemon juice.

Serve on dessert dish (2 is about right) and add topping.

Sprinkle almonds over top. Serves: 8.

Wine Cake

1 yellow cake mix
1 package vanilla pudding mix
1 teaspoon Schilling nutmeg
3/4 cup Wesson vegetable oil
3/4 cup cooking sherry
4 IGA California eggs

Dana Moore
Sacramento, CA

Heat oven to 350°.

Beat ingredients on high speed for approximately 4 minutes.

Pour batter into a greased, bundt, cake pan.

Bake for 40 minutes. Cool.

Sift powdered sugar over top of cake after removing from pan. Serves: 14

Nectarine, Plum & Raspberry Crisp

Margie Tose

Paragarys/Capitol Grill

Cafe Bernardos

Margie Tose is a graduate of the Calif. Culinary Academy. Her speciality is desserts. The biggest influence for Margie was her mother and the time spent in the kitchen. This recipe is from those moments in the kitchen with her mom. Margie is the pastry chef for Paragary's/Capitol Grill and Cafe Bernardo's

3 pounds nectarines, cut in two-inch chunks
2 pounds plums, cut in two-inch chunks
1 basket raspberries, fresh
6 tablespoons flour
1 cup IGA sugar

Streusel Topping:
1 cup brown IGA sugar
2 teaspoons Schilling cinnamon
1 cup flour
1 cup cornmeal
1/2 pound unsalted butter, cold

In a large bowl combine fruit, flour and sugar. Toss well. Place in a 9 x 13 glass pan. Proceed with topping.

Place all streusel ingredients in a mixer with paddle attachment and mix until coarse meal looking. Or you may use a food processor using pulsing turns. Sprinkle topping over fruit and bake at 350° oven for approximately one hour or until bubbly and streusel is lightly browned. Serve crisp warm with vanilla ice cream. Serves: 12.

Peach and Pecan Bread Pudding (double recipe)

Madams Rouge's

24 slices French bread (about 3/4 inch thick)
1 cup Crystal butter, melted
8 cups half-and-half
2 1/2 cups IGA sugar
20 IGA California egg yolks
2 teaspoons vanilla extract
2 pinches salt
8 large peaches, peeled, pitted, and thinly sliced
2 cups toasted pecan halves
vanilla Crystal ice cream or whipped cream, for accompaniment

Preheat oven to 425° Brush bread with some of the melted butter. Put bread slices on a baking sheet and bake until golden brown (about 10 minutes).

In a medium saucepan over medium-low heat, bring half-and-half to a simmer (bubbles will appear at edge of pan). In a large bowl, beat sugar with egg yolks; whisk hot half-and-half into egg-sugar mixture. Stir in vanilla and salt; set aside.

Pour remaining butter into two 9x13-inch baking dishes. Place 6 bread slices in each dish; strain half of egg-custard mixture; top with pecans. Arrange remaining bread over fruit and strain remaining egg-custard mixture over bread. Let stand 1 hour, covered with plastic wrap, or refrigerate up to 6 hours.

If refrigerated, remove from refrigerator about 2 hours before serving. Preheat oven to 325° Bake, uncovered, until golden brown and slightly crusty, (about 1 3/4 hours). Serve warm, cut into squares and topped with vanilla ice cream or whipped cream.

Chocolate Cake

Senator Tim Leslie

Senator Tim Leslie was elected to the Senate in 1991, after serving in the Assembly and before that, in both local government and private industry. Married to Clydene, with daughter, Debbie, and son, Scott.

2 cups flour
2 cups IGA sugar
2 sticks Kraft margarine
4 tablespoons cocoa
1 cup water
1/2 cup buttermilk
2 beaten IGA California eggs
1 teaspoon soda
1/2 teaspoon Schilling cinnamon
1 teaspoon vanilla

Topping:
1 stick Kraft margarine
4 tablespoons cocoa
6 tablespoons Crystal milk
1 cup chopped nuts
1 teaspoon vanilla
2-2 1/2 cups IGA powdered sugar

Mix flour and sugar in bowl. In saucepan mix margarine, cocoa and water. Bring to boil and pour over flour and sugar. Mix well. Add buttermilk, eggs, soda, cinnamon and vanilla. Beat well and bake for 20 to 30 minutes in 400° oven.

For topping bring margarine, cocoa and milk to a boil. Remove from heat and add nuts, vanilla and powdered sugar. Spread on cake about 5 minutes after taking from oven.

Mud Pie

1 cup flour
1/2 cup chopped nuts
1/2 cup Crystal butter
8 ounces soft Kraft cream cheese
1 cup IGA powdered sugar
1 cup whipped topping
1 small package vanilla instant
  pudding
1 1/2 cups Crystal milk
1 small package chocolate instant
  pudding
1 1/2 cups Crystal milk
shaved unsweetened chocolate.

Marcie Stamm
Sacramento, CA

To make crust; mix flour, butter and nuts like pastry. Press into bottom of 9x13-inch inch pan and bake for 10 minutes. Cool.

Next layer: mix softened cream cheese, powdered sugar and Cool Whip. Spread over crust, then layer vanilla instant pudding mixed with milk and spread over cheese, powdered sugar and whipped topping layer.

Spread instant pudding (chocolate) mixed with milk (according to box instructions) and spread over vanilla pudding layer.

Spread rest of whipped topping on top and sprinkle with shaved unsweetened chocolate. Serves: 12

Cherries 'n Cream Squares

Crust:
1 1/4 cups graham cracker crumbs
1 1/2 tablespoons IGA powdered sugar
2 ounces Kraft margarine, melted

Filling:
6 ounces Kraft cream cheese, softened
3/4 cup IGA powdered sugar
1/4 tablespoon vanilla
1 1/4 cup miniature marshmallows
1 1/4 cup whipped topping
2 cups cherry pie filling
1/8 teaspoon almond extract

Terri Miladinovich
Acampo, CA

Combine crust ingredients; press into bottom of pan; refrigerate. In large bowl beat cream cheese, powdered sugar and vanilla until light & fluffy.

Fold marshmallows and whipped topping into cream cheese mixture. Spread mixture over crust. Add almond extract to pie filling.

Spread over cream layer. Refrigerate several hours or until firm.

Pan size; 6x8-inch. Cut 3x4 (or 2-inch squares) 239 calories per square. Serves: 12

Tiramisu

Agnese Roccucci

I have worked at Vincenzo's Restaurant here in Stockton for 14 years as an Assistant Chef. I was born and raised in Italy and came to America in 1960. I have a passion for cooking Italian dishes.

1 container of mascarpone cheese
6-8 large IGA California eggs
Espresso Coffee
Chocolate, grated enough to sprinkle on top
2 packages lady fingers
6-8 tablespoons IGA sugar
1 ounce rum (optional)

Make a full pot of espresso coffee in espresso coffee pot. Let cool completely.

Add rum (optional) after coffee has cooled.

Separate whites from yellows on eggs. Beat whites until stiff. Beat yellows, sugar, and mascarpone cheese until you get the color of the mascarpone cheese.

Fold egg mixtures together.

In a casserole dish: make first layer by dipping lady fingers into coffee and layering bottom of dish with them.

For second layer put a layer of mascarpone mixture.

The third layer is lady fingers dipped in coffee. Continue until dish is full ending with cheese mix. Sprinkle grated chocolate on top.

Refrigerate and serve. Serves: 10-12

Chocolate Chip Bundt Cake

1 package devil's food cake mix
1 package instant chocolate
   pudding
1 (12-ounce) package chocolate
   chips
1 3/4 cups Crystal milk
2 IGA California eggs

Mary Adams
Sacramento, CA

Grease and flour bundt pan. Combine all ingredients in bowl, mix by hand until well blended, about 2 minutes. Pour into bundt pan. Bake at 350° for 50-55 minutes. DO NOT overbake. Cool 15 minutes in pan, remove and continue cooling on rack. Sprinkle with powdered sugar. Serves: 9-10

Fruity Yogurt Shake

1 8-ounce carton nonfat plain yogurt
1 8-ounce can crushed pineapple
   packed in its own juice*
1 medium or large ripe banana
   (some brown spots should be
   visible in the peel)
3 tablespoons IGA sugar
dash Schilling nutmeg
10 ice cubes

Debra Sampson Boogaard
Folsom, CA

Place all ingredients in a blender in the order listed. Blend until ice cubes are thoroughly crushed (about 1 minute). Serve immediately. Serves: 2-3

* Substitute 8 ounces fresh strawberries, if desired; omit the nutmeg.

Nona Louisa's Biscotti

Diana Lowery

This recipe was my grandmother Louisa's creation. This cookie is a loved favorite of every generation. Diana is a public awareness consultant who loves to cook, shop, and travel.

1 1/4 cube Crystal butter
3/4 -1 cup IGA sugar
Cream above ingredients
3 large IGA California eggs
3 cups flour
3 teaspoons baking powder
1/4 cup vanilla (pure)

Cream all ingredients. Form long rolls 2 1/2 -3" wide on Pam sprayed baking sheet. Rolls can be as long as pan. Bake at 350° until semi-firm, slice at a diagonal, and return cookies to oven until golden on each slice. Simply wonderful with coffee, tea or wine. Serves: 2 dozen

Willie Brown's Rice Pudding

Willie Lewis Brown, Jr.

Willie Lewis Brown, Jr., Democrat, Speaker of the Assembly for the state of California. First elected November, 1964.

1/4 cup uncooked rice
1/3 cup IGA sugar
1 quart Crystal milk
1/2 teaspoon vanilla
grated nutmeg

Mix all ingredients together in a glass baking dish. Top with grated nutmeg. Bake 1 hour at 350° stirring mixture under at 15 minute intervals. Remove from oven when top browns thoroughly. Cool and serve.

Adill Spencer's Simple Pound Cake

1 pound Crystal butter (softened),
    DO NOT use margarine!
1 box IGA powdered sugar
6 IGA California eggs
3 cups flour
1 teaspoon vanilla
1 teaspoon lemon extract
1/2 cup Crystal milk

Geri Spencer Huntz
Sacramento, CA

Preheat oven to 350°.

Cream butter and sugar together until smooth.

Alternate adding eggs and flour (add eggs one at a time, beat thoroughly after each addition).

Mixture should be smooth and thick, add flouring, and milk, beat well.

Pour into greased, floured, bundt pan.

Bake 350° until done. Remove from pan immediately. Serves: Many

Walnut Pie

2 tablespoons Crystal butter or Kraft margarine
1 cup IGA brown sugar, packed
2 tablespoons flour
1 cup light corn syrup
3 IGA California eggs, well beaten
1 cup walnut meats (coarsely chopped)
1 teaspoon vanilla
3/4 teaspoon salt
1 unbaked 9" pastry shell

Preheat oven to 400°. Work butter in a bowl until creamy. Stir in sugar and flour. Mix well. Add syrup and eggs. Beat until mixture is fluffy. Stir in nuts, vanilla and salt. Pour mixture into uncooked pie shell. Bake 15 minutes. Lower heat to 350° and bake 30-35 minutes longer. Center will be soft, jellylike. Serves: 6-8

Vicki Spannagel
Penryn, CA

Health Bar Cookies

1 small box Rice Krispies
an equal amount of corn flakes
1 cup (generous) chopped walnuts
1 cup (generous) shredded coconut
1 cup IGA white granulated sugar
1 cup white Karo syrup
1 cup Crystal heavy cream

Cook slowly to the soft-ball stage. Pour over the dry ingredients. Spoon into foil or colored cupcake holders. Use your imagination and decorate each Health Bar Cookie. Kids love them. Grown-up's like them too.

Royden Noyes Cornell
Sacramento, CA

Butterscotch Chip Cookies

1/2 cup shortening
1/4 cup IGA sugar
1/2 cup IGA brown sugar
1/2 teaspoon vanilla
1/2 teaspoon almond
1 IGA California egg
1/2 teaspoon baking soda
1 cup plus 2 tablespoons flour
1/2 teaspoon salt
1/2 cup chopped Macadamia nuts
1 cup butterscotch chips

Cream shortening, sugar and flavorings until light. Add egg and beat. Sift flour, soda and salt. Add to creamed ingredients. Stir in nuts and chips. Bake on greased sheet. 10 minutes at 375°

Fern Freel
Sonora, CA

Turtle Cake

1 package German chocolate cake mix
1/2 cup evaporated milk
1 (14-ounce) package Kraft caramels
3/4 cup Crystal butter or Kraft margarine
3/4 cup chopped pecans
1 (12-ounce) package chocolate chips
1 cup pecan halves (approximately 36)

Flora M. Kinmore
Stockton, CA

Preheat oven to 350°. Prepare cake mix according to package directions.

Pour 1/2 of batter into a greased 9x13-inch pan. Bake only 15 minutes.

In top of double boiler over hot water, melt together caramels, evaporated milk and butter. Pour 1/2 of caramel mixture over baked portion of cake.

Sprinkle chopped pecans and 1/2 package of chocolate chips over caramel mixture. Spread remaining cake batter over caramel mixture.

Bake an additional 25 to 30 minutes.

After cake has cooled slightly, spread rest of caramel mixture over cake and top with pecan halves and remainder of chocolate chips. Serves: 18

Luxury Lemon Bars

Larry N. Vanderhoef

Larry N. Vanderhoef is the Chancellor at UC Davis. He was born in Minnesota, reared and married (Rosalie) in Wisconsin. Larry learned to play squash in Illinois. With nest (Susan, 24; Jon, 20) now empty, life is ... wonderful!

Crust:
2 cups flour
1/2 cup IGA powdered sugar
1 cup Crystal butter

Filling:
4 IGA California eggs
2 cups IGA granulated sugar
4 tablespoons flour
1 teaspoon baking powder
2 regular lemons (cannot be Meyer lemons)

To make crust: Mix all ingredients until smooth. Press into 9 x 13" pan and pat up sides. Bake 15 minutes at 350°. Let cool.

For filling: Grate yellow surface skin of lemons into mixing bowl. Then add juice of the lemon and the rest of the ingredients.

Mix together, pour into cooled, pre-baked crust. Bake 25 minutes at 350°. Cool.

Dust with powdered sugar. Serves: 12

Apple Dip

9 Granny Smith apples
2 jars butterscotch caramel ice
   cream topping
2 (8-ounce) packages Kraft cream
   cheese
salted peanuts

Mix 1 jar topping and cream cheese. (Microwave 1 minute to soften) Spread on 12x16-inch tray. Sprinkle on salted peanuts. Spread remaining topping on top. (Microwave 1 minute in jar to soften) Slice apples and soak for at least 1 hour in 7 Up. Arrange apple slices on ends of tray.

Janet L. Berreth
Lodi, CA

Almond Spice Bar Cookies

3/4 cup Crystal butter or Kraft
   margarine
1 cup IGA sugar
2 IGA California eggs, unbeaten
1/4 cup molasses
2 cups flour
2 teaspoons baking soda
1 teaspoon Schilling cinnamon
3/4 teaspoon cloves
3/4 teaspoon powdered Schilling
   ginger
1 cup slivered almonds

Mix butter or margarine with sugar, eggs and molasses. Sift flour, baking soda, cinnamon, cloves and ginger. Then add almonds. Add dry ingredients to the first mix. Stir (the batter will be stiff). Pour into a well greased 9x13-inch pan. Bake 20-25 minutes until the center tests done with a toothpick. Cut into bars while still slightly warm. Store tightly closed when cold.

Margaret M. Wilner
Auburn, CA

Heart Healthy Brownies

1/2 cup boiling water
1/2 cup unsweetened cocoa
   powder
1 1/2 cups IGA sugar
1/3 cup Wesson corn oil
1 teaspoon vanilla
4 IGA California egg whites, room
   temperature
1 1/4 cups all-purpose flour
1 teaspoon baking powder
1/4 teaspoon salt (optional)
3/4 cup chopped walnuts

Oven: 350° Spray: 8x12-inch or 9x9-inch baking dish with vegetable spray.

In large bowl, combine boiling water and cocoa. Mix with a wire whisk until well blended and smooth. Add sugar, oil, vanilla, egg whites, flour, baking powder and salt. Mix well with whisk, Fold in nuts. Bake: 25 minutes. Serves: 8

Emily A. Moulton
Carmichael, CA

Sinfully Rich Fudge Brownies

Consuelo Maria Callahan

Connie Callahan is a Superior Court Judge for San Joaquin County. She is currently presiding over the criminal department. Connie is married and has two teenage children. Connie comes from a family of chocolate lovers. This is a favorite family recipe, especially with the kids.

4 ounces unsweetened chocolate
1 cup Crystal butter
4 IGA California eggs
2 cups IGA sugar
1 tablespoon vanilla
1/4 teaspoon salt
1 cup flour

Frosting:
4 ounces unsweetened chocolate
1 cup Crystal butter
2 IGA California eggs
1 tablespoon vanilla
1 pound package IGA powdered sugar
4 cups mini marshmallows

Preheat oven to 350°. Grease 9x13-inch pan. In large sauce pan, combine chocolate and butter. Heat over low heat until melted and smooth, stirring occasionally. Remove from heat. Beat in eggs, sugar, vanilla, and salt until blended. Stir in flour. Spread evenly in bottom of greased pan. Bake 25-30 minutes. Should be moist. Do not overbake. Cool in pan.

Prepare chocolate marshmallow frosting. Refrigerate several hours overnight. Cut chilled brownies into bars. Store in refrigerator. Makes: 40 brownies

Pumplesauce

2 cups pureed fresh pumpkin (DO NOT USE CANNED PUMPKIN)
4 medium golden delicious apples, peeled, cored, cut into small chunks
1/4 cup water
3/4 teaspoon vanilla
1/4 teaspoon Schilling cinnamon
3 tablespoons IGA granulated sugar
3 tablespoons IGA brown sugar
dash Schilling nutmeg

Debra A. Sampson Boogard
Folsom, CA

To puree pumpkin. Cut pumpkin in half and scoop out all seeds and stringy pulp. Cut pumpkin into chunks and, using a paring knife, cut off rind. Cut pumpkin into 2" chunks. Steam chunks -7 minutes or until tender. (Boiling the pumpkin will make it too watery; baking it will make it too dry.) Puree steamed pumpkin in food processor until smooth. Note; You can freeze the puree in 2-cup containers to make this recipe long after pumpkins are in season.

To cook the apples. Bring apple chunks and water to a boil, cover and simmer 5-10 minutes, until apples are tender. Stir in remaining ingredients and simmer an additional minute.

Transfer cooked apples to a bowl and mash with a fork (or puree in food processor if a smoother consistency is desired). Stir in pureed pumpkin. Serve hot or cold!

Spicy Lemon Peanut Butter Cookies

Rochelle Clipper

Rochelle is a Head Start teacher who works part-time preparing delicious nutritious meals for the children of First Step Crisis Nursery in Stockton

1/2 cup Crystal butter
3/4 IGA granulated sugar
3/4 firmly packed IGA light or dark
    brown sugar
1 cup peanut butter
1/2 teaspoon vanilla and lemon
    extract
1/2 teaspoon Schilling cinnamon
1/2 teaspoon baking soda
1 1/4 cups flour (unsifted)
1/2 teaspoon salt (optional)

Preheat oven at 375° Grease cookie sheet lightly. Mix dried ingredients together. Beat butter, sugars, eggs, peanut butter and cinnamon together until creamy. Add dry ingredients to mixture. Mix well.

Shape into small ball, size of a walnut, then place on cookie sheet. Press with back of fork making a cross design.

Bake cookies for 8-10 minutes until golden brown.
Serves: 30

Lemon Custard Cake

1 prepared angel food cake (10
    inches)
1 package (3.4-ounce) instant
    lemon pudding mix
1 1/2 cups cold Crystal milk
1 cup (8-ounce) Crystal sour cream
1 can (21-ounce) cherry or straw-
    berry pie filling

Mrs. Edwina Bitterman
Lodi, CA

Tear the angel food cake into bite size pieces.

Place in a 9x13-inch pan.

In a mixing bowl, combine the pudding mix, milk and sour cream.

Beat until thickened, about 2 minutes. Spread over cake. Spoon pie filling over top.

Chill until serving time. Serves: 12-16

Grandma's Pound Cake

1 cup Shortening
3 cups IGA sugar
5 IGA California eggs
1 cup Crystal milk with 1 teaspoon
    baking powder mixed in
1 teaspoon vanilla
1 teaspoon lemon
1 teaspoon almond
3 cups flour
1/4 teaspoon salt

Elizabeth McCleary
Sacramento, CA

Mix sugar, Crisco and eggs (adding eggs one at a time and mixing between each).

Add milk mixture and extracts. Sift in flour and salt. Beat until smooth, about 2 minutes.

Pour into ungreased 2-pound tube pan.

Bake at 350° for about 1 1/2 hours.

Delta Mud Pie

1 1/4 cups flour
1/2 cup cocoa powder
2 teaspoons baking soda
1/2 teaspoon salt
1/2 cup IGA sugar
1 cup packed IGA brown sugar
1 cup Crystal butter
1 teaspoon vanilla
2 IGA California eggs
1 (12-ounce) package chocolate
   chips
2 cups oatmeal
1 cup walnuts

Teresa M. Angle
Stockton, CA

Preheat oven to 350°.

Combine flour, cocoa, baking soda and salt; set aside.

In separate large mixing bowl, beat butter, sugars and vanilla until creamy.

Add eggs one at a time and beat well after each egg.

Add flour gradually, beating continuously. Stir in chocolate chips, oatmeal and walnuts.

Drop by tablespoon onto ungreased cookie sheet.

Bake 10-12 minutes. Let cookies cool five minutes before removing from sheet. Makes: 3-4 dozen

Chocolate Roll

1 1/2 cups IGA powdered sugar
4 IGA California egg yolks
3 tablespoons cocoa
3 tablespoons flour
1/2 teaspoon baking powder
pinch of salt
4 IGA California egg whites
1/2 teaspoon cream of tartar

Barbara Chilton
Roseville, CA

Beat powdered sugar with egg yolks until light and fluffy.

In separate bowl mix cocoa, flour, baking powder and salt. Whip egg whites with cream of tartar until stiff.

Fold 1/2 of each together and then combine gently but thoroughly.

Spread on slightly oiled waxed paper on cookie sheet.

Bake approximately 25 minutes at 350°.

Dampen dish towel slightly and sprinkle with powdered sugar.

Let cake cool for 5 minutes then remove from pan.

Peel off waxed paper and roll up in cloth and let cool that way.

Unroll later and fill with sweetened whipped cream. Roll up again and frost with chocolate frosting. Serves: 8

Magic Peach Cobbler

1 stick Kraft margarine
1 cup IGA sugar
1 cup flour
1 1/2 teaspoons baking powder
3/4 cup Crystal milk
1 3/4 sliced peaches
1 cup IGA sugar to top peaches

Sandra G. Reed
Columbia, CA

Use a 9x13-inch baking pan and melt cube of margarine in 350° oven. Mix sugar, flour, baking powder and milk. Pour over melted margarine. Do Not stir. Add peaches on top of mixture. Sprinkle with remaining sugar. Do Not stir. Bake at 350° for 30-40 minutes. May substitute berries or apricots for peaches.

The Preventor's No Bake Peanut Butter Cookies

The Preventor

2 cups IGA sugar
1/2 cup Crystal milk
1/4 cup Crystal butter or Kraft
  margarine
4 tablespoons cocoa
3/4 cup chunky peanut butter
3 cups of quick oatmeal
1 teaspoon of vanilla

Combine the sugar, milk, butter and cocoa in a pan; bring to a boil and boil for 1 minute.

Remove from heat and add peanut butter, vanilla and oatmeal. Mix together and place spoonfuls on waxed paper. Let cool. Enjoy!

Lemon Sauce

1/2 cup Crystal butter
1 cup IGA sugar
1 1/4 cups water
1 well-beaten IGA California egg
3 tablespoons lemon juice

Myra G. Burris
Modesto, CA

Combine in a small sauce pan and cook 5-6 minutes over medium heat. Stir constantly until mixture comes to a boil. Use over gingerbread, Jello, or bread pudding. Serves: 6-8

Fudge Nutty Brownies

Jai Baker — Awful Annie's

I have been interested in the culinary field for years. I have received many awards for dessert recipes and "Jain Hollywood Chili." I have owned Awful Annie's Restaurant in Auburn for 3 years.

1 cup Kraft margarine, melted
2 cups IGA sugar
1 cup flour
2/3 cup powdered baking cocoa
1/2 teaspoon baking powder
2 IGA California eggs
1/2 cup Crystal milk
2 teaspoons vanilla extract
1 cup chopped pecans or walnuts

Frosting:
2 teaspoons vanilla
1 (12-ounce) package semisweet chocolate chips
1 (14-ounce) can sweetened condensed milk

Preheat oven to 350°. Combine all brownie ingredients except nuts; beat 2 minutes with mixer. Stir in nuts if desired. Spread in greased 9x13-inch baking pan. Bake 40 minutes or until brownies begin to pull away from sides of pan. Just before brownies are done, over low heat, melt the frosting ingredients. Stir until glossy and smooth, about 1 minute. Immediately spread over hot brownies. Cool. Cut into bars. Makes: 12-16

Black Forest Torte

Into large mixing bowl, mix:
1 3/4 cups flour
1 3/4 cups IGA sugar
1 1/4 teaspoons soda
1 teaspoon salt
1/4 teaspoon baking powder
2/3 cup soft Kraft margarine
4 squares (1 ounce each) Baker's unsweetened chocolate, melted and cooled
1 1/4 cups water
1 teaspoon vanilla
3 IGA California eggs

Pam Nelson
Auburn, CA

Heat oven to 350°. Brush sides and bottoms of four 8" round pans. Line bottoms of pans with waxed paper.

In large bowl combine flour, sugar, soda, salt, baking powder, margarine, melted chocolate, water and vanilla. Beat 2 minutes at medium speed. Add eggs. Beat 2 more minutes. Pour 1/4 of batter into each pan. Bake 15-18 minutes. Toothpick inserted in center of each layer will come out clean. Cool slightly, remove from pan. Cool completely.

For chocolate filling: melt 1 1/2 bars (4 ounces each) Baker's German sweet chocolate. Cool. Blend 3/4 cup soft margarine. Stir in 1/2 cup chopped almonds.

For cream filling; beat 2 cups whipping cream with 1 tablespoon sugar and 1 teaspoon vanilla.

To complete - 1 layer of cake, 1/2 of chocolate filling, 1 layer of cake, 1/2 of cream filling, repeat having cream filling on top. Do not frost sides. Decorate top with chocolate curls made with remaining chocolate bar and chopped nuts.

Melba Laub's Peach Cobbler

Dough:
1/4 cup soft Crystal butter
1/2 cup IGA sugar
1 cup sifted flour
2 teaspoons baking powder
1/4 teaspoon salt
1/2 cup Crystal milk

Topping:
1 1/2 quarts sliced peaches or
  peaches from No. 2 can
1/4 - 1/2 cup IGA sugar
1 cup juice from peaches

Emma Lea Dorris
Rocklin, CA

Heat oven to 375°. Cream together butter and sugar until fluffy. Sift dry ingredients - add to creamed mixture with milk. Spread dough in bottom of baking pan, then drain 1 1/2 quarts peaches or peaches from no. 2 can (reserving 1 cup juice). Spread sliced peaches on top of dough. Sprinkle with 1/4 to 1/2 cup sugar. Then pour 1 cup fruit juice over top. Bake 40-50 minutes.

Blackberry Custard Torte

Geno Duggan - Captain Jon's

While doing some hiking in the Calavares County mountains, I found some wild blackberries. At that time the idea for this delicious torte came upon me.

Crust:
1 cup all-purpose flour
1/2 cup IGA sugar
1 1/2 teaspoons baking powder
1 stick (1/2 cup) cold unsalted
  butter, cut into bits
1 large IGA California egg, lightly
  beaten

Custard:
2 cups Crystal sour cream
1/2 cup IGA sugar
1/4 teaspoons vanilla
3 large IGA California egg yolks
4 cups blackberries, picked over

To make crust: In a bowl with a pastry blender or in a food processor blend or pulse together flour, sugar, baking powder and butter until mixture resembles meal. Add half of egg and toss or pulse until incorporated, adding remaining egg if necessary to just form a dough. Form dough into a disk and chill, wrapped in wax paper, 1 hour.

To make custard: In a bowl whisk together all custard ingredients until smooth.

To assemble torte: Preheat oven to 325° and butter a 9-inch spring form pan. Wrap foil around bottom and halfway up side of pan.

On a lightly floured surface roll out dough into an 11-inch round and fit it into bottom and 2 inches up side of prepared pan. Arrange 2 cups blackberries on crust and pour custard over top

Bake torte in middle of oven 1 1/2 hours, or until custard is set, and cool in pan on rack. Remove side of pan and top torte with remaining 2 cups blackberries.

181

Appetizers

Soups & Salads

Vegetarian Main Dishes & Vegetables

Meat, Poultry & Fish

Main Dishes

Holiday Recipes

Desserts

Order Form

To reserve your copy(s) of <u>California Heartland Recipes</u>, benefiting the Child Abuse Prevention Councils of Sacramento, Placer, and San Joaquin Counties complete this form, making your check or money order payable to <u>California Heartland Recipes</u>.

I would like to reserve _____ copy(s) at $19.95 each $_____

(plus shipping, tax & handling of $3.95 per book) $_____

Special multiple order rates for shipping:
(5=$15, 10=$25, 15=$40, 20=$50)

Total amount enclosed is... $_____

Charge my Mastercard_____ or Visa _____

Card # _____ Exp. Date_____

Signature_____

(credit card orders only)

Ship Cookbook(s) to:

Name _____

Address _____

City _____ ST ____

Zip _____ Phone _____

Please use the enclosed response envelope or mail to:

California Heartland Recipes
c/o KXTV Channel 10
400 Broadway
Sacramento, CA 95818

Order Form

To reserve your copy(s) of <u>California Heartland Recipes</u>, benefiting the Child Abuse Prevention Councils of Sacramento, Placer, and San Joaquin Counties complete this form, making your check or money order payable to <u>California Heartland Recipes</u>.

I would like to reserve _____ copy(s) at $19.95 each $_____

(plus shipping, tax & handling of $3.95 per book) $_____

Special multiple order rates for shipping:
(5=$15, 10=$25, 15=$40, 20=$50)

Total amount enclosed is... $_____

Charge my Mastercard_____ or Visa _____

Card # _____ Exp. Date_____

Signature_____

(credit card orders only)

Ship Cookbook(s) to:

Name _____

Address _____

City _____ ST ____

Zip _____ Phone _____

Please use the enclosed response envelope or mail to:

California Heartland Recipes
c/o KXTV Channel 10
400 Broadway
Sacramento, CA 95818

Order Form

To reserve your copy(s) of <u>California Heartland Recipes</u>, benefiting the Child Abuse Prevention Councils of Sacramento, Placer, and San Joaquin Counties complete this form, making your check or money order payable to <u>California Heartland Recipes</u>.

I would like to reserve _____ copy(s) at $19.95 each $_____

(plus shipping, tax & handling of $3.95 per book) $_____

Special multiple order rates for shipping:
(5=$15, 10=$25, 15=$40, 20=$50)

Total amount enclosed is... $_____

Charge my Mastercard_____ or Visa _____

Card # _____ Exp. Date_____

Signature_____

(credit card orders only)

Ship Cookbook(s) to:

Name _____

Address _____

City _____ ST ____

Zip _____ Phone _____

Please use the enclosed response envelope or mail to:

California Heartland Recipes
c/o KXTV Channel 10
400 Broadway
Sacramento, CA 95818